A Russian Moment

Produced by Copyright Studio

Production: Jean-Paul Paireault
Design: Jacqueline Leymarie
Photo Research: Anna Obolensky and Jean-Paul Paireault
Translation: Josephine Bacon

CLB 2661
© 1991 Colour Library Books Ltd, Godalming, Surrey, England.
Photographs © 1991 A.N.A.
All rights reserved.
This 1991 edition published by Portland House,
distributed by Outlet Book Company, Inc, a Random House Company,
225 Park Avenue South, New York, New York 10003.
Color separations by Tien Wah Press (PTE) Ltd, Singapore.
Printed and bound in Singapore.
ISBN 0 517 05309 8
8 7 6 5 4 3 2 1

A RUSSIAN MOMENT

PHOTOGRAPHS:
LEONID BERGOLTSEV
VADIM GIPPENREITER
ANATOLI GORIAÏNOV
NICOLAI RAKHMANOV
MARK STEINBOCK
VLADIMIR SVARTSEVITCH
LEV WEISMAN

CAPTIONS:
BORIS FIALKOVSKY

INTRODUCTION:
BILL HARRIS

PORTLAND HOUSE

My great adventure began the day that Vladimir Potapov came into my office. A photographer himself, Vladimir represents Moscow's Union of Graphic Artists, to which Russia's independent photographers belong, and he was suggesting that we collaborate on a project using these photographers. Perestroika was just beginning: the Berlin Wall was coming down, Central Europe was rebelling, and Russia was opening up. Vladimir's proposal was a timely one, and I was very eager to get to know the land of my ancestors better.

We set out for Moscow in search of photographers whose work would reveal the many and varied aspects of the vast country that is Russia. Sadly, the poor-quality film and second-rate camera equipment that were all they had at their disposal meant that we were unable to use material from some of the many talented photographers we met.

Among those we could use, our first find was Lev Ilich Weissman, who has worked for twenty years in Siberia and who is passionate about the ecology and ethnography of Arctic Russia and Siberia. We were the first people to be shown his photo-essay on the flora and fauna of Wrangel Island; that essay would later be published throughout the world. Lev has also published several photographic works in Russia. Our second discovery was Nicholas Rakhmanov, who was born in Moscow in 1932. He worked for Tass before becoming a photojournalist for the Sunday supplement of *Izvestia*. He has traveled throughout Russia, where he is well known thanks to his many books, including *Treasures of the Kremlin, Leningrad, Moscow, The Bolshoi Theater* and *A Journey through Russia*.

Next we met one of Russia's photographic giants, Vadim Levgenievich Gippenreiter. Born in the year of the revolution to a noble father and a peasant mother, Vadim is a fit man who still dons a rucksack to go up into the Caucasus Mountains to take photographs. With twenty-two photographic books to his credit, Vadim is well known in Russia and is a photographer of enormous versatility.

Other finds were Mark Steinbock, a photojournalist for the magazine *Ogoniuk*, who contributed essays on daily life in Russia; Vladimir Svartsevich, a talented photojournalist with *Izvestia*, who contributed some powerful photographs on the theme of Perestroika, together with articles on Gorbachev, Yeltsin and Sakharov; and Leonid Bergoltsev, President of the Photographers of Moscow, whose contribution included historic photographs of Khrushchev's last days in power and of the beginning of the Brezhnev era.

Among the young photographers we met was Anatoly Goriaïnov, who is already an important figure at only thirty-four. A photographer with a painter's eye, he began taking photographs in 1985 and has since had his work exhibited and published – he has a great talent and a great future. Other talented young photographers we met were Alexander Stepanienko and Pavel Maximienkov.

From the thousands of photos that we viewed we selected those that would recreate a visual moment in the life of this vast country, as captured by her best photographers. Our thanks go to them and to all those who helped us, believed in us and trusted us.

Anna Obolensky

Princess Anna Obolensky

CONTENTS

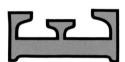
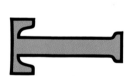

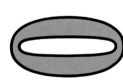

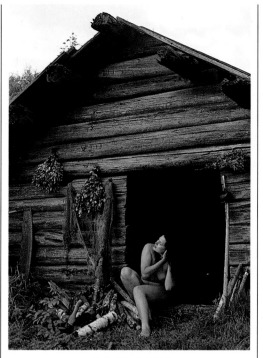

SOCIETY

NATURE

TOWNS

REPUBLICS

GLASNOST

INTRODUCTION

The United Nations does its work in six different languages, and in the nearly fifty years since it began helping to make the world smaller hundreds of words have become interchangeable in all of them. But in recent years, Russia has contributed a word to the international language that many Russians themselves only dreamed of using a half-century ago.

The word is *perestroika*. Roughly translated, it means "restructuring," but freely translated it stands for one of the most dramatic series of changes that have taken place in any country in the lifetime of most of the world's people. The outcome still remains to be seen, of course, but it has created an astounding moment in Russian history.

Credit for the shift in Russia's outlook belongs to Mikhail Sergeyevich Gorbachev, who became General Secretary of the Communist Party, the *de facto* head of the Soviet Government, in March, 1985. Like the changes he would begin implementing right away, he himself represented a change that surprised many of the experts on both sides of the Kremlin Wall. Most of them had considered him too young. Though Josef Stalin became General Secretary at forty-five and his successor Georgi Malenkov had been fifty-one, the five men who followed them during the next thirty years were all over sixty. Mr. Gorbachev was only fifty-four, and almost all his colleagues in the Politburo, the fourteen men with the power to decide who would have absolute control over the 287 million citizens of the Soviet Union, were old enough to be his father.

If Gorbachev represented a kind of youth movement, he was hardly wet behind the ears. He had become a member of the party's Central Committee fourteen years earlier and was in charge of party affairs in the Stavropol region, a favorite place among the Communist hierarchy for rest and rehabilitation. It put him in a position of close association with the people who could encourage a young man able to play the tricky game of politics, and Mikhail Gorbachev was a master at it. But even if the party bosses didn't have a fascination with the health spas in the Caucasian Mountains, Stavropol is also an important farming district, and was a center of attention in the 1960s, when Premier Nikita Khruschev was experimenting with ways to make collective farms more productive. Gorbachev, already head of the Communist youth organization for the entire district, became one of the chief organizers of the scheme and enrolled in a night school to enhance his law degree with another in agriculture.

The Khruschev experiment was a dramatic success in Stavropol if not elsewhere, and in 1978 Gorbachev went to Moscow as Party Secretary for Agriculture. As one of the youngest men in the national leadership, other young men gathered around him, and over time he managed to build a following, especially among intellectuals who considered him one of their own. The political leadership was also impressed, including Yuri Andropov, the chief of the KGB, who became his mentor. When Andropov took charge of the government in 1982, he was sixty-eight years old and too ill to participate in the day-to-day demands of the job. He made Gorbachev his deputy, and though the younger man carefully followed the General Secretary's orders as he ran the country by proxy, Andropov also encouraged him to organize his own personal brain trust into committees that could suggest reforms for the future. It was a perfect springboard for Gorbachev's future, too, and when Konstantin Chernenko replaced Andropov two years later Gorbachev was allowed to continue his planning. More important, the seventy-two year-old Chernenko also deferred to the younger Gorbachev, who went right on running meetings of the Politburo and the Party Secretariat. When Chernenko died, the Old Guard died with him, and Mikhail Gorbachev became the first Soviet leader born after the 1917 Revolution.

PETER THE GREAT

Both his detractors and his supporters often compare Gorbachev to Peter the Great, who ruled Russia in the first quarter of the eighteenth century, and who to this day is still a controversial figure. Peter became Czar at the age of ten when his half-brother, Feodor, died in 1682. Very much like Andropov and Chernenko, Feodor had spent most of his six years of rule virtually on his deathbed, and not unlike Gorbachev, the boy who replaced him had spent those years laying a foundation for the future. Like many youngsters, little Peter enjoyed playing soldiers, except in his case he played with real ones. He hadn't been Czar very long when an uprising took place and his older half-sister, Sophia, who probably started the uprising herself, assumed the title of Regent and further clipped Peter's wings by insisting that his brother, Ivan, should share the title of Czar.

None of it seemed to bother Peter, who was free to live in the country, play with his soldiers and to learn from members of a small foreign community nearby. Among the things he discovered on one of his estates was an English-built boat which, quite unlike any other in Russia, was able to sail either with the wind or against it. He had it refitted and mastered the art of sailing, and with the knowledge began to dream a dream that would change Russia forever.

He managed to have Sophia banished to a convent when he was seventeen, and at the same time Ivan, whose poor health had caused him to be passed over in the first place, stepped down and left Peter in complete control. But the Czar preferred the company of foreigners to his own people, and spent the next several years learning all he could about the Western world. He also put the Russian peasants to work building a fleet of sailing ships which stood him in good stead in an encounter with the Turks at Azov in 1696. It gave Russia a port that led to the Black Sea and markets to the south, but the Sultan of Turkey let it be known that he considered the sea his private lake and though Russia was strong and Peter determined, the Turks were a force to be reckoned with. Peter's answer to the problem was to send a delegation of ambassadors on a tour of the countries of Europe. He himself went along, becoming the first Czar ever to leave Russia, but because he wanted to use the opportunity to study and learn he decided to go in disguise. He probably didn't fool anyone. Czar Peter was six feet, seven-and-a-half-inches tall.

Their announced mission was to explore the possibility of forming an alliance among the European powers to defeat the Turks. But they were also looking for ideas to help restructure the Russian way of life, a seventeenth-century version of Perestroika but without the openness that Gorbachev would one day call *glasnost*. As it turned out, the European monarchs had no stomach for taking on the Turks, so the Czar turned his attention to finding ways to do it himself. When he reached Amsterdam, the Dutch East India Company humored him by giving him a job in one of its shipyards, and before he left several months later he had learned every job in the place and could easily have got work as a marine architect if he hadn't had other things to do. His fellow workers were enthusiastic about the shipbuilding skills of the English and so he rushed off to London to learn even more. But he did more than just learn. During his months in Holland and England, he signed hundreds of his teachers to long-term contracts and sent them back to Moscow to pass their knowledge along to potential shipbuilders among the Russians. He had planned to spend a few months in Venice to learn from the recognized masters of the shipbuilding art, but another revolt forced him to go home again. Before long, he would create a Venice of his own.

He arrived back in Moscow a changed man, and began a program to change his countrymen as well. The Russians had traditionally thought of themselves as an Asiatic people, but Peter decided they should be more European, as he himself had become. He started by ordering all the men to shave off their beards and to cut off their long robes to knee length. Anyone who resisted was given a free shave and clothing alteration by the Czar's soldiers. Peter also scandalized the traditionalists be decreeing that the new century would officially begin on January 1, 1700, rather than on September 1, which had always been New Year's Day in Russia.

His next step was to make his army more European. He himself had formed two Western-style regiments as a follow-up to the games he had played as a youngster, but there was work to be done with the rest of his army. He accomplished it in three months by conscripting men from every segment of society, treating nobles and serfs as equals in a rigorous training program that bordered on cruelty. He didn't have the time for any other way. Peter wanted ports on the Baltic and no price was too high to pay. Most of the coast was under the thumb of the King of Sweden, and even though he had recently negotiated a peace treaty with him, Peter formed an alliance with Poland, Denmark and the German state of Brandenburg to bring Sweden to its knees. The Russian troops went down in defeat, but rather than continuing the attack, the Swedish King marched on to Poland, leaving the Russians time to recover. Not content with simply rebuilding his army, Peter sent his men to the poorly-defended Baltic coast and took the Swedish fortress at the mouth of the Neva River.

When he joined them there, he shocked everyone by announcing that he intended building a city on the marshy islands they had taken and that it would be his new capital. The site was desolate. It was on open water, hundreds of miles from any other city. There was no shelter nearby and no food for the thousands of men he put to work there, not to mention no tools for them to work with. The war with Sweden had barely begun and the workers were in constant danger of attack. But no matter what, an order from the Czar was not something to be ignored, and no one questioned what they were being asked to do, though there were very few who didn't think that Peter was touched with madness. Thousands died building his great city, but palaces and cathedrals rose over their graves, and Czar Peter was so pleased with the result that he toyed with the idea of calling it Paradise before naming it St. Petersburg in honor of his personal patron saint.

While the work was going on, the Swedes defeated the Poles, and as they were turning their eyes toward Moscow, there were rebellions along the Volga and among the Cossacks of the Don. Their ranks were swelled with peasants who had joined them to resist the prospect of forced labor and military conscription, and the Swedish King decided to use the rebels to help him beat Russia from the inside. The result was that his army was trapped on the windblown steppes when winter arrived. Peter's army caught up with them the following summer and easily defeated them at Poltava, sending their king into exile. After that, the Russians eliminated their enemies one by one. All that is, except the Turks. But if the Black Sea was still off limits, Peter kept up his war with the Swedes, and though it took him ten years, he finally gained control of the Baltic and was proud to note that victory had come through "ships built with our own hands." He was equally proud that those ships had brought security to his beautiful city of St. Petersburg.

The government was already functioning there by the time the war ended. Merchants and craftsmen had long since been ordered to move north to St. Petersburg from Moscow, along with the families of the nobles whether they wanted to live there or not. Very few of them did. It was cold and damp, and though it represented Russia's transformation in the eyes of the world from a country of barbarians to a partner in the European community, it was in the heart of the wilderness. But Peter shared his countrymen's love of glitter and gaiety and hardly a day went by when there wasn't a masquerade, a ball, a parade, a fireworks display, all of which gave them something more to talk about than the weather.

As a way of showing their gratitude, the nobles and patriarchs gave him the new titles of Emperor, Father of his Country and the Great. The ordinary people, however, were burdened with heavy taxes and were subject to forced labor, and little love was lost between them and the Czar. But no one in the country worked harder than he did, and though his methods were oppressive, all the work was, in Peter's opinion at least, being done for the benefit of the people. He sincerely wanted to turn the Russians into a prosperous nation, and it was the only way he knew. He had given them ports to trade with Europe, but they had nothing to trade but raw materials that merchants across the sea turned into more profitable manufactured goods which were often sent back to Russia at high prices. As he had done with shipbuilding, Peter hired foreign experts to teach his people to become factory workers. He noted that Russia was more blessed than most other countries with minerals, and so he encouraged mining and the building of foundries. But he also felt that "our people will not do anything new unless they are forced to it," and he never shrunk from the use of force without mercy. Peter had always been fascinated by education, and forced that on his people, too. He ordered that no man would be allowed to get married until he could read and write and had mastered arithmetic and geometry.

Many overtaxed peasants breathed a sigh of relief when Peter the Great died in 1725 at the age of fifty-two, but all Russia knew that it had lost a leader who had been much larger than life. He had built the army to an almost invincible force of a quarter-million men. He had created a navy of more than eight hundred ships where none had existed before and had given it an outlet to the seas of the world. Better still, he had given them a new, modern capital with a window on the Western world. And the Western world had taken notice.

THE BYZANTINE INFLUENCE

But if Peter had changed Russia, changing the Russian people was a different matter. They were the product of centuries of outside influences that began in 862 A.D., when Viking warriors known as Varangians established themselves on the shores of Lake Lagoda and took it on themselves to become the protectors of the scattered Slavic tribes that were already there. After establishing themselves at Kiev, these men who called themselves "men of Rus," decided to attack Byzantium, the Eastern survivor of the Roman Empire. Their savage attacks on the countryside around the Bosphorus prompted the Byzantine Emperor to negotiate a treaty with them. This allowed the Russians to trade with them as long as they followed strict rules that restricted their visits to small groups, allowed only in the summer months. Those who went there were mightily impressed by the opulence of the Byzantines, and before long began entertaining dreams of attacking the place again and having it all to themselves. But for all their savagery and power they failed. It took a woman to make Byzantium and Russia partners. Grand Princess Olga had succeeded her husband, Igor, when he was murdered by his own subjects who thought he had been too greedy in extracting tribute from them. Then, after quickly avenging his death, she put on all her finery and headed toward the Byzantine court to be received as the head of a neighboring state.

Olga went home to Kiev with rich gifts and a pledge of eternal friendship from the Emperor Constantine, the most powerful ruler in the world at the time, but she also took a more subtle gift back to her people. She had been baptized a Christian. The Slavs weren't quite ready for Christianity, though, and over the next several decades the tribes kept on routinely fighting among themselves with very little thought about religion of any kind. But her grandson, Vladimir, who eventually became Russia's ruler, had a passing interest in the subject. When he defeated the Bulgars, they tried to interest him in becoming a Moslem, but he refused to entertain the thought because they frowned on drinking, and he knew that his people would never forgo that pleasure for God or any man. At the same time, Christians from Germany tried to convert him, but in spite of his grandmother's experience, he resisted them, too. The Khazars of the Volga region told him of their Jewish religion, but he rejected them, too, because their God was too vengeful for his taste.

The Byzantines turned all that into an opportunity. They invited Vladimir for a state visit and arranged for the most colorful mass ever to be celebrated in the Cathedral of St. Sophia. The impression was everlasting. Vladimir was baptized with all the pomp and ceremony Byzantium could muster, and when he went back to Kiev he ordered all his people to follow his example. He also took the Emperor's daughter as his wife, binding his kingdom with the Byzantines and bringing their brand of civilization to his people along with their religion.

THE RISE AND FALL OF THE TATARS

In the years that followed, Kiev became as opulent as Constantinople itself, and Russia was unified under its new god and the descendants of Vladimir, who became the stuff of heroic legends, very much like those told of King Arthur and Charlemagne. But after about 250 years another towering figure emerged on the scene. This was Genghis Khan, the leader of a fierce tribe of Mongols the Russians knew as Tatars. By the time he died in 1227 he had the dubious distinction of having conquered more territory and killed more people than any man who ever lived; a record that still stands. Russia herself was one of the victims, but the death blow wasn't struck until after the Great Khan himself had died. The Mongols attacked in 1240 and swept across Russia destroying farms and villages as well as cities, and it was said that "no eye was left open to weep for the dead." When it was all over Kiev itself had been destroyed, and Russia was under the absolute control of the savage Tatars for another two hundred years.

It broke apart the fragile unity of the Russians, but time and a taste of civilization also drove a wedge into the resolve of the Tatars themselves. Meanwhile, out on the steppes, men with no allegiance to either side in the series of wars and feuds that followed had banded together for the sheer pleasure of fighting. If these men – who called themselves Cossacks – had any enemy at all it was the Tatars, and because they fought from horseback in the same way as the Tatars, they were able to give a good account of themselves. In time their ranks swelled by tens of thousands, and what had started as a band of adventurers became an army of Christians dedicated to driving the Moslem Tatars out of their country, though they didn't mind fighting against their Russian brothers when there were no better enemies in sight.

The Cossacks' moment of glory came when the Turks conquered Byzantium. The Tatars fell into lock step behind the Turkish Sultan and all of Europe was threatened, but the Russian guerilla army went out of its way to insult him. And the princes who controlled a big piece of Russia from Moscow took advantage of the situation to expand their holdings, and to make Moscow Constantinople's successor in the role of keeper of the faith and the center of the Orthodox Church. Grand Prince Ivan made it a reality by marrying Princess Sophia, the niece of the last Emperor of Byzantium. He reunited the provinces and cities, creating the largest country in Europe, and marshalled an army that ended Tatar rule. He also invited builders from abroad to rebuild Moscow itself. Among them was the great Italian Renaissance architect Aristotle Fioravanti, who designed the fortress walls of the Kremlin as well as the Uspenski and Arkhangelski cathedrals and the Granovitaya Palace. All of the work was in the Byzantine style, and the ceremonies that became traditional in the Russian court were carefully taught to the nobles by Princess Sophia herself.

Their grandson, Ivan IV, was only three years old when his father died, but when he was thirteen he took power into his hands, ending squabbling among the rich landowners by sentencing the most powerful of them to death as a warning to the others. Two years later he announced that he wanted to be crowned Czar of all the Russias, and made the title meaningful by leading an army to drive the last of the Tatars from his domain. In the process he turned the Volga into a Russian river and opened trade routes to the East across Asia. But in the last twenty-four years of his life he changed from the savior of his people into a kind of monster, remembered to this day as Ivan the Terrible. He tortured and killed his people by the thousand, and organized an efficiently-run secret police network to protect him from any opposition. Even his own bodyguards weren't safe from the steel-tipped spear he always had at his side, and it came as a surprise to no one when he used it during a fit of violent temper to kill his own son, the heir to the throne. But during his reign his empire grew, and in his last year the Cossacks defeated the Tatars in the north and added the forests of Siberia to its territory.

Future Czars would find Siberia a convenient place for exiling the families of men who offended them. One of them, Boris Godunov, once even ordered the clapper of a bell that offended him removed and sent off to the frozen north. But Siberia also became a haven for many Russians. No one in the country was safe from calamity and despair; not even the gentry were safe from sudden arrest, torture and death. But the ones who suffered most were the peasants who, though they formed an overwhelming majority, were among the most oppressed people on earth, even during the Middle Ages. But in those earlier days they were better off than most of their European counterparts, allowed to rent the land they farmed with freedom to leave it as long as their harvest was in and they were free of debt. Their lot began changing in the seventeenth century when, ironically, life among the peasants of Europe began to improve.

SERFDOM IN RUSSIA

In expanding their territories, the early Czars became the sole owners of huge stretches of countryside, and they used the land to reward nobles who helped them in time of war. But they only granted the use of the land, retaining ownership themselves. Knowing that their estates would probably not be passed along to their heirs, the landlords tried to get all they could from it during their own tenure by raising the rents and demanding more productivity. Meanwhile, the Czar, as the actual owner, also demanded payment in the form of taxes levied directly on the peasants, and required them to make themselves available for any work required by the State, such as roadbuilding, as well as for military service. Many of them cut their losses by moving to land controlled directly by the Czar, which eliminated the rent payment but left them wondering if the Little Father in Moscow might, in a sudden fit of generosity, reward one of his faithful servants with their own farm. Peasants could also settle on the millions of acres of tax-free lands owned by the Church, and many did. But the monks charged them rent, too, and also took the profits from their surplus produce, as well as turning them into virtual slaves responsible for all the physical work of the religious communities.

There was yet another option open to them. They could run away. And when rich lands in eastern Russia were made safe many migrated there and lost themselves in the luxurious tall grass of the steppes. Thousands more went deep into Siberia, where the Czar's men couldn't find them and take them back to suffer punishment as runaway debtors. Many of those joined the ranks of the Cossacks, who proudly proclaimed that they would never serve any master nor pay any taxes, and they had the means of backing it up.

The tide was stemmed with a new law that required all peasants to be registered and strictly forbidden to leave the land for any reason. Many peasants still managed to escape into Siberia, but for all practical purposes the law gave more power and control to the government than even the most ambitious Czars had ever dreamed of. It was promulgated at the beginning of the Romanov Dynasty, during the reign of Czar Michael, and proved to be the seed that would end Romanov rule with the Communist uprising in 1917.

The gulf between rich and poor grew dramatically in the nineteenth century. The ideas and dreams that Peter the Great had brought in from the West were difficult for the lower classes to accept, and generally had a greater effect on the gentry who were better educated, and were made to feel even more superior than they had in the past. Peter also changed the rules of serfdom by imposing a tax on peasants based on a census that was to be held every twelve years. It counted babes in arms along with octogenarians as well as able-bodied men, and the tax was based on the total count in each village, which remained the official number until the census taker came around again. The tax bound serfs together because in many families a man who had been counted might subsequently have died or been sent off to war, or may not yet have become old enough to contribute any income. The serfs were already forbidden to move so they bound themselves together in communes. Their resources were divided equally among them and every family contributed what it could to pay the taxes. The Czar had absolute power over all his people, but nearly half of them regulated their own lives, as long as they paid their taxes and maintained a low profile.

They were officially known as Crown peasants and, though they were comparatively free by the standards of eighteenth-century Russia, their lives were hardly their own. They belonged to the Czar as surely as the horses in his stables, and they never knew when they might be forced to abandon their villages and move hundreds of miles with their neighbors to some alien place the government decided needed development. If they protested, Cossacks, who were no longer freedom fighters, were sent in to destroy their homes. Then insult was added to injury in the form of special taxes to pay the expenses of the Cossacks. They were also subject to becoming the private property of some noble as a gift of the Czar to one of his favorites.

More than forty-five million Russian peasants were slaves to the gentry in the 1790s. As happens in all forms of slavery, there were many benevolent masters and some serfs lived comfortable, prosperous lives even though they were not free, but most were made painfully aware that their owners had the power of life and death over them. This majority led miserable lives that often ended in agonizing death.

CATHERINE THE GREAT

It was a time when slavery was becoming a thing of the past in the West, but it was on the increase in Russia during the reign of Catherine the Great, who decreed that all the peasants of the Ukraine, families that had been born free, were classified as serfs. And during her thirty-four year reign that began in 1762, hundreds of thousands were given up into slavery.

Even more than Peter the Great, Catherine was responsible for bringing Western influences into the Russian court. It was only natural, for she had come from the West herself. She had gone to Russia as a teenage girl to fulfil a marriage contract with Grand Duke Peter, the future Czar. In her eighteen years as Grand

Duchess she developed a strong affection for Russia that was in direct proportion to her dislike of her husband, a dullard who was generally despised by his people. Even before he became Emperor, she had involved herself romantically with several army officers who later helped her engineer the arrest and death of the monarch, making her Empress in his place. She landed running. She intrigued with Frederick the Great to divide Poland between them and used the rebuilt Russian fleet to bring the Turkish Sultan to his knees. By the time she was finished, her adopted country had dramatically expanded its borders and even the Black Sea was open to Russian shipping for the first time. But for all the good she did for Russia, she also brought suffering to the people whose taxes financed her programs and made her court the most glittering in all of Europe.

The world changed dramatically, too, during Catherine's reign. Revolutions in the United States and France had swept away old ideas and the people had taken control of their own destiny in England. Her son, Czar Paul, did what he could to reverse the trend and send his country back to the Dark Ages, and he may have succeeded if *his* son, Alexander, hadn't arranged to have him murdered. As Czar himself, Alexander began planning new reforms that included unheard-of ideas such as freedom of speech and jury trials. He even hoped to do away with serfdom. But he was up against centuries of tradition and, like many leaders, he found it easier to involve himself in international affairs than to deal with conflicting ideas at home. And events on the international scene at the beginning of the nineteenth century were well worth his attention.

ALEXANDER AND NAPOLEON

After the French Revolution, European monarchs began worrying about losing their heads, as had happened to Louis XVI, and began a series of wars that lasted nearly twenty-five years. The French army emerged from them as the most powerful in Europe, and its commander, Napoleon Bonaparte, began dreaming of controlling the entire continent. By the time Alexander became Czar, Napoleon had made himself First Consul, one of the three men who ruled France. He had already conquered Austria and Italy and was well on his way to making his dream come true. Alexander joined the fight against him, but when his armies were badly mauled, he decided to join him instead, and Napoleon welcomed the opportunity. But not many Russians were sure the Czar had made a smart move. They were forbidden to trade with England, which had been Russia's most important customer, and their young men were forced to fight in Napoleon's armies, even though Russia herself was embroiled in another war against the Turks. Napoleon wasn't too happy with the arrangement, either, as it turned out. Russian merchants had persuaded Alexander to lift the embargo against the English, which infuriated the French. But more important, Napoleon was not the sort of man who enjoyed sharing power. Convinced that blockading the Baltic would bring the hated English to their knees, he took the matter into his own hands by massing his troops for an attack on Russia in 1812.

Half the Russian army was still in Turkey and the other half was split inside Russia itself. Napoleon's plan was to conquer the country before they could regroup. But, as he marched across the Russian landscape, he met no opposition and saw very few defenders. Towns and villages were deserted and crops and other supplies that could help an invading army had either been destroyed or removed. It was springtime, and the weather was either hot or frosty and spring rains turned the roads to mud. Napoleon's Grand Army pressed on, but by the time they engaged the Russians, more than half their soldiers had already been lost. Neither side could claim a solid victory in any of the battles that followed, but by the fall the retreating Russians had led Napoleon to Moscow itself.

Nothing could have buoyed the army's spirits more than the sight of the great city and Napoleon was overjoyed. He sent an advance guard to demand the key to the capital, but it turned out they didn't need one. When the French soldiers marched into Moscow they found nothing but silent streets. Lamps were burning in houses and candles blazed in the cathedrals, but there was no sign of life anywhere, not even household pets. The entire population of Moscow, more than 250,000 men, women and children, had vanished, just as their retreating army had many times before. As Napoleon was making himself at home in the deserted palace behind the Kremlin walls, his men went about systematically looting the city. But before long they had another distraction: Moscow was on fire. The wind-driven flames engulfed the city for four days, and by the time a rainstorm quenched them, ninety percent of the city was in ruins. Napoleon's men were more devastated than ever and he began calling for peace, but there was no one to hear him. The Czar and his generals were nowhere to be found. A few weeks later, Napoleon made a fateful decision. Rather than spending the winter in Moscow, he decided to head back to Paris. He had been warned about the severe Russian winter, but it was the middle of October and there was no sign of it anywhere.

Winter came a little late to Russia in 1812. But it arrived with a vengeance about two weeks after the French army began heading south. The troops were burdened down with loot they had gathered, but they left most it behind by the side of a road that couldn't be seen in the deep snow. They also left their own supplies behind, and by the time they reached the border, they had also left the corpses of half their comrades. The army that had come into Russia with five hundred thousand men left it with less than fifty thousand. And during the seven weeks it took to retreat from Moscow, though they saw Cossacks off in the distance, they never saw any other Russians nor heard any sounds except for the baying of packs of dogs that followed them.

Like nothing else could, Napoleon's experience in Russia served as a warning to other armies, and the Russians were more secure than ever before. Czar Alexander had become an important world leader and his country was no longer regarded as a nation of barbarians. Russia's borders had been expanded and its wealth increased. But Alexander's presence on the world stage had no effect whatever on the lives of ordinary Russians. Most of them were still serfs and still suffering in silence.

Alexander didn't pick up many fresh ideas in his travels around Europe, but the men of his army did. They were exposed to the freedom of the French Republic and had watched the Greeks, their spiritual brothers, declare their independence. They had discussed the results of the revolution in America and seen the early effects of the industrial revolution in England. But when they went back home again, they found that nothing had really changed in Russia. A man could still be banished to Siberia for a minor infraction, thousands of families were still living in slavery, and the Czar still answered to no one.

When Alexander died suddenly with no heir, some of the army's top officers took it as an opportunity to catch up with ideas that had been sweeping Europe for decades. The Czar had designated his brother Nicholas as his successor, but a group of radicals decided that the crown belonged to another brother, Constantine, and let it be known that even he would not be acceptable without a constitution giving power to the people. They backed up their demand by leading a battalion of soldiers into Moscow in December, 1825, but after they had spent several hours milling around the Senate Square waiting for their leaders to decide what to do next, Nicholas ordered his soldiers to fire on them. Hundreds were killed and the survivors were thrown into prison. Several months later, five of them were hanged and more than one hundred others exiled for life. The revolt of the so-called Decembrists was over and life went on as before. But the demonstration hadn't been quite the same as other little revolts the Russians had seen before. For the first time, it wasn't peasants revolting against the aristocracy, but a part of the aristocracy itself revolting against the system. It was something to think about.

THE ABOLITION OF SERFDOM
(IDEAS OF FREEDOM)

But for the moment there was something more important to think about. In an effort to take control of Turkey, Czar Nicholas had blundered Russia into war with England and France, a conflict known as the Crimean War. When it lost the war, its first defeat in a century and a half, Russia was forced to give up its treasured rights to the Black Sea. It also lost its image of invincibility in the eyes of the world, and on the home front the intellectual community began questioning the practice of keeping ninety percent of the population in slavery. Nicholas died before the war ended, and his son, Alexander, assumed the crown with a promise that there would be reforms. Chief among his ideas was the abolition of serfdom, but it raised more questions than it answered. All his ministers and advisers were landowners themselves, and it was a bitter pill for them to swallow. But a Czar doesn't have to follow anyone's advice, and in 1861 Alexander freed the serfs. Landowners were forced to give up a percentage of their holdings, which were turned over to the village communes. The former owners were to be compensated for their loss by the government, which would recover the funds though annual mortgage payments paid by the new owners, an idea that helped the Czar keep the peasants bound together in communal groups and kept them from moving away. Not every peasant was better off than before, but they were no longer slaves. Alexander also protected their rights by allowing jury trials and establishing regional governments to give the people a voice in their own affairs. It was the most dramatic change that had taken place in Russia since the Byzantines had given it Christianity, but Russia wasn't out of the woods yet. The Czar still had absolute control over the lives of everyone.

The peasants were still tied to the same communes. They had a voice through their local councils, but no one had to listen and often no one did. Most peasants had less land than before, and they were often forced to pay rent for enough additional land to survive; and the mortgage payments for the land they theoretically owned were layered on top of the already oppressive taxes they had been paying all their lives. Some of them did very well, to be sure, and became entrepreneurs within their communes, lending money at high rates of interest to their neighbors and generally behaving exactly like the landlords that had been eliminated. And even if every other aspect of the scheme had been perfect, few former serfs could ever accept the idea that the land shouldn't have been given to them outright in the same way it had been divided among the gentry since the beginning.

Such ideas festered among student groups in the 1870s, and young people by the thousands went out from the comfort of the university campuses to try to organize the peasants and convince them to fight for meaningful change. In most cases their pleas fell on deaf ears, and hundreds of them were sent off to Siberia for their trouble. But they also carried on a guerilla war, in spite of the harsh punishment that faced them if they were caught. It came to a head in 1881, when a student tossed a bomb at the Czar, killing both Alexander and himself.

The assassination convinced his son, Czar Alexander III, that his father had been too liberal, and he became more oppressive than any of his predecessors had been. And he wasn't content to restrict his harsh rules on just his own people. Poland, Finland and Turkey had become Russian vassal states, and he extended his iron fist in the direction of their people as well. They were forced to adopt Russian as their official language, and it was quite clear that everyone needed to be careful about what they had to say. The underground terrorists, who called themselves "The People's Will," continued to function, but their situation seemed more hopeless than ever.

The fight inside Russia was against ideas that had evolved over centuries and had long since become a seemingly irreversible fact of life. At the same time, other Europeans were looking for a way out of a new kind of oppression. The industrial revolution had hugely increased the ranks of a class of people who owned nothing and survived by working for wages paid by other people who had as much control over their lives as any landowner ever had over his serfs. Such people had been part of every society since the ancient Romans gave them the name of proletariat, but at the beginning of the nineteenth century they became a majority, and intellectuals began wrestling with ideas to put an end to their misery. In Germany, philosophers Karl Marx and Friedrich Engels crystallized the socialist idea that all the means of producing the necessities of life should be owned by all the people, rather than being controlled for the profit of a few. Other philosophers had put forward such ideas before, but Marx and Engels wrote that the time had come to do more than discuss such things. The system needed to be changed, they said.

Such ideas fell on fertile ground in Russia, where the new concept of a classless society seemed to be the only way to stop the tide of history. Most of the Russian people were still farmers and didn't quite fit the traditional definition of proletariat, but enough of them had become factory workers to create a substantial underground of revolutionaries who branched out all over the country, quietly preaching the new gospel. Many were exiled and many more thrown into prison, but the Czar considered them relatively harmless. He thought of them as eggheads whose ideas would eventually fade away. And because they weren't preaching violence as others had, he didn't make a strong effort to force them out of existence.

He was firm with them, though, and when Vladimir Ulinov began publishing a newspaper aimed at the working class, he was arrested and exiled to Siberia. Life there wasn't too hard for him. He even managed to arrange to have a fellow revolutionary sent there to join him and then married her. They wrote a book together and signed it with his revolutionary name, Nikolai Lenin.

They were released in less than five years, and went to England to resurrect his newspaper, which he called "Spark." The flames would come later. The revolutionary underground had split over principles during the years he was away, but he considered himself the leader of the largest number of them and gave his movement the name Bolshevik, from the Russian word *bolshinstvo*, meaning "majority." He was wrong. The majority was actually on the other side, but he was about to get a boost from the Czar himself.

REVOLUTION

It had become traditional for Russian Czars to expand their country's borders and Nicholas II turned his eye in the direction of Manchuria and Korea, which would give him ice-free ports on the Pacific. But before he could make a move, the Japanese moved against him, and after eighteen months of fierce fighting drove the Russians back. During those months the Czar's own world was falling apart. The people, faced with inflationary prices and oppressive working conditions, were at the edge of open rebellion. In 1905, after sending him a petition that explained " … we are at the end of our strength," nearly two hundred thousand, led by their clergy, marched on the winter palace. But, instead of an audience with the Czar, they were met by gunfire from the palace guard. Hundreds were killed and hundreds more wounded. The revolution had begun.

The massacre was followed by a general strike and a wave of terror that included the assassination of the Czar's uncle. Nicholas cooled the situation by instituting an Imperial Duma made up of representatives of the people directly elected by them. But the same decree also stipulated that only property owners would have the right to vote, and that the Czar would not be bound by any recommendations the Duma might make. The proletariat was still out in the cold. More strikes and more demonstrations forced Nicholas to give the new council more power, but over the next several years he quietly took back what he had given, and by 1912 many of the dissidents in the socialist movement had come around to the Bolshevik point of view, and though he wasn't actually in Russia, Nikolai Lenin held the future of his country in his hands.

But the Bolsheviks still didn't represent a true majority and events in Europe were sending Russia headlong toward a future that might easily have been controlled by men with other ideas. When Germany declared war against Russia in 1914, Austria and Turkey followed suit, and the Russian army lost four million men in less than a year. Czar Nicholas took the situation into his own hands and went off personally to take command at the front, even though he knew very little about military matters. While he was away, his wife, Alexandra, took charge of the government and in less than a year managed to earn the animosity of workers and gentry alike.

Whatever they may have thought of her, though, the people had nowhere else to turn when they were faced with a severe bread shortage in the winter of 1917. Hundreds of thousands of them marched on St. Petersburg, which had recently been renamed Petrograd, demanding bread. Cossacks were called out to stop them, but instead they joined the demonstrators. A few days later, during an even larger demonstration, whole regiments defected and, together with the people, stormed police stations and prisons and sacked the arsenal to provide them with more weapons. Then they approached the Duma and offered to protect it from the autocracy. The Duma responded by creating a special committee, a soviet, to establish a new government.

Within a week, Czar Nicholas abdicated. The revolution was over. The new soviet was composed of landowners and even a few nobles, not exactly the answer to a revolutionary's dreams. But they gave the people undreamed-of freedoms and released all the political prisoners. They also began forming other soviets in other cities to take over the government. But they didn't have a clear mandate. There were still other factions to be heard from.

THE ESTABLISHMENT OF COMMUNISM

First among them was Lenin's Bolsheviks, but Lenin himself was still out of the country, and a competing socialist faction that called itself Mensheviks had made one of its own head of the Petrograd Soviet. When Lenin returned in the spring he pointed out that credit for the revolution belonged squarely with the Petrograd working class, but that they had put the soviet in the hands of the intellectuals and it, in turn, had turned the government over to the bourgeoisie, the very men who, in his opinion, had the potential of oppressing workers. His job, as he saw it, was to give the revolution back to the people who had created it – the working class.

They were already proving their ability by running individual soviets in all parts of the country, and they were proving to be a thorn in the side of the Provisional Government. But they were, by and large, Mensheviks, and Lenin knew that if his Bolsheviks were to prevail, there was work to be done. He suffered a strong setback when rumors began spreading that he was actually a German agent. Lenin felt strongly that Russia had no business fighting the war against Germany and by repeatedly saying so he found himself accused of breaking down the morale of Russian soldiers. The opposition took advantage of the situation and sent Lenin into hiding after sending his chief lieutenant, Leon Trotsky, to prison. Neither of them was out of sight for long. An election a few months later gave the Bolsheviks a majority in Petrograd, and Trotsky was set free to become Soviet Chairman. Lenin slipped back in disguise and convinced his followers that the time had come to take the government by force.

They planned their revolution carefully. Trotsky managed to get the support of all the army regiments in Petrograd and ordered them to hold themselves on alert. He took charge of the Peter and Paul Fortress, and his followers at Kronstadt commandeered the cruiser Aurora, and planning to anchor it within gun range of the Winter Palace. When all was in place, they quietly began seizing parts of the infrastructure. During the night of October 24, they took charge of the telegraph office and the electricity power plant; they quietly replaced the workers controlling the water supply and even took over the government's bank. Having done all that, they interrupted radio broadcasting with the announcement that the Provisional Government no longer existed and that power had passed to the Bolsheviks.

Some of the officials quietly left town and the others stoically waited for Lenin's followers to drop the other shoe. Their next obvious move was to take control of the Winter Palace, but the cruiser didn't arrive until the day was nearly over. When it did, the conspirators picked up the telephone and ordered the ministers inside to surrender. When they refused, the big cannon at the fortress began firing and the guns of the Aurora joined in. Bolshevik soldiers followed the barrage by storming the palace, and a few hours later the ministers who had run the Provisional Government joined the Czar's own minions behind the walls of the Peter and Paul Fortress.

It is one thing to declare a new government and quite another to make it real. The Bolsheviks had promised a free election, but in spite of the name they had given themselves, they still didn't have the support of the majority of the people. Of the 700 members of the Assembly that met a few months later, only 175 were Bolsheviks. But that didn't prevent them from proposing that it should rubber-stamp all the Bolshevik policies. When the delegates refused, the Bolsheviks marched out of the room and, after the meeting was adjourned, they went to work to blockade the palace and barred the door to everyone except the Bolsheviks themselves. In the weeks that followed, they formed their own Congress and their policies became the only law in Russia.

The changes were as dramatic as the Revolution itself. All vestiges of class distinction were swept away. The homes and palaces of the former gentry were converted to offices and apartments to serve the workers. Government support of the church was eliminated and its educational institutions abolished. Family structures were broken down and women given absolute equality, able to work while their children were cared for in public institutions. Education was encouraged, and was provided free, as was all medical care.

But human nature being what it is, even such Utopian ideas didn't get overwhelming acceptance. The Bolsheviks were far from a majority and they had put themselves in a position of changing the life of every Russian citizen.

Even Lenin himself recognized the fact that his followers didn't represent the majority, and he changed their name from Bolsheviks to Communists when he moved the government from Petrograd to Moscow. And because he knew all about the power of words, he also instituted the strictest censorship the Russians had ever seen. The new leaders put teeth into their edicts by organizing secret police to root out counter-revolutionary thought, and before long the prisons they had emptied were getting new tenants. They also kept ordinary citizens in line by making it impossible to buy food without a special identity card, which the police could confiscate for any perceived crimes against the new State.

It was obvious to Lenin that even those measures weren't strong enough to impose his ideas on an entire country, and one of his top priorities was building up a Red Army. His opponents had organized themselves against him, and had encouraged foreign governments to support them. By the middle of 1919, buoyed with the promise of outside help, their so-called White Army, largely an outgrowth of the old imperial forces, went on the offensive. The civil war that followed was one of the bloodiest Russia had ever seen, but by the time it was over, the Reds were firmly established and the foreign armies that had crossed into Russia during the world war had all gone home. More important, the dedication of the Red Army to make changes in the Russian way of life, compared to the Whites who were perceived as defenders of the status quo, helped win new converts to the Communist cause.

But the people were still suffering. Lenin relaxed some of his demands on them and before he died in 1924 he was generally perceived as a genuine hero of the Russian people, who gave him the high honor of renaming the city of Peter the Great "Leningrad." His successors did a little name changing of their own, renaming Mother Russia the Union of Soviet Socialist Republics, sending a message to the world that they considered their revolution international and that they expected other countries to be united with them.

As far as they were concerned, history began in 1917 and Russia no longer existed. Ironically, however, even as they were ignoring the lessons of their history they were in many ways repeating it. The Czars were gone and the lives of the people had changed, but the new rulers were as oppressive in their own way as the emperors had been in theirs. But for all the change they brought, the old Russia still shines through, and at this moment in its history it is the symbols of the past that fascinate the rest of the world.

RUSSIA OLD AND NEW

Leningrad is a mecca for visitors, not because it is the cradle of Communism but because it is the city of Peter and Catherine. Decembrist Square is a memorial to the 1825 uprising against the Czar, but it is dominated by a massive statue of Peter the Great. St. Isaac's Cathedral is a museum today, but it is a constant reminder of the great power of the Orthodox Church in another time, and it is guarded by a statue of Czar Nicholas I. And the world-famous Hermitage, which ranks along with the Louvre in Paris and the Metropolitan Museum in New York, stands along with the Winter Palace as a memorial to Catherine the Great.

In Moscow, the Kremlin is international Communism's most important symbol. It was where Lenin lived after the Revolution and where he worked to create the Soviet Union, and it is where his mausoleum was built. But the fortress itself was built in the fifteenth century and is as important to the history of Czarist Russia as it is to the Communist era.

The Kremlin is a collection of buildings on a sixty-nine-acre site surrounded by a sixty-five-foot-high brick wall. It was the place where all the Czars were crowned and where they lived when they were in Moscow, and it was also the official headquarters of the Russian Church, which had three cathedrals inside the walls. The cathedrals are museums now, as is the Grand Kremlin Palace; all reminders of a glittering past that wasn't swept away and is still as much a source of pride to the Russians as ever.

Both Moscow and Leningrad are in the Russian Republic, the largest of the fifteen separate Republics of the Soviet Union. It has nearly fifty-two percent of the country's population and covers seventy-five percent of its territory. The Ukrainian Republic, third largest in area, but second in population, is the place where Russian history began. Its great city of Kiev is where Christianity came to Russia from Byzantium, where culture arrived in books and manuscripts from Greece, and where the Cyrillic alphabet was introduced to translate them into the Slavonic language. There are probably more churches in Kiev than in any other Soviet city and its St. Sophia Cathedral is a masterpiece of Byzantine art. As in other cities of Russia there are plenty of monuments to the new way of life, but the past dominates the spirit as strongly as it does the skyline.

And now, even the recent past is history. Perestroika seems to be changing everything. They talk of getting the people involved in politics, but the average Russian thinks of politics the way the rest of the world feels about the weather: you may be allowed to talk about it, but there isn't much you can do to change it. But the winds of change are, indeed, blowing hard in this moment of Russian history. And if the Russian people themselves have been made apolitical by centuries of absolutism, the whole world is watching in fascination to see where Mr. Gorbachev's restructuring will lead them. But no one on the outside looking in is quite ready to declare that the idea of freedom and democracy will change Russia forever. Every step of the way through their history, the Russian people have found that freedom is always followed by greater oppression, and that taking part in the democratic process has usually given their oppressors a weapon to use against them. Though the Communists have denied all history before 1917, the entire history of the Russian people is very real to all of them. On the other hand, thousands of Russians have become active in the support of all kinds of causes, from saving the environment to sharing a love of rock 'n roll music. Many hard-liners in the Party see them as a threat and, in a way, they might be right. The Revolution itself grew out of discussions among working class people who had gathered together for quite different reasons than political activism. They finally seized the moment and changed their world. The current younger generation in Russia could, quite possibly, change the course of history again. They have already begun, in fact. It isn't uncommon for groups of people, including staunch party members, to speak out against their local officials, and for the first time in the memory of any of them, there is no need to look over their shoulders when they do. It is giving them self-respect, and to many Russians, indeed to people everywhere, the feeling is habit-forming. The government itself has estimated that environmentalists have effectively blocked more than a thousand projects in a two-year period, and the traditional party bosses are losing elections in district after district, giving the Party a headache in finding new jobs for them. But just as a robin doesn't make a spring, the ice hasn't melted yet, and the next chapter in Russian history is still a blank page.

SOCIETY

Traditional baptism near Moscow.

Sauna in a village in northern Russia.

The great affection which grown-ups have for the young is partly due to the difficult times which previous generations have experienced since 1914, especially those who lived through the German occupation. The traditional sollicitude which the peoples of central and southern Asia have for their offspring is also well known. A child has eleven years' schooling before attending college. Throughout this period, he is surrounded by the Communist party organisation, first as a "pioneer" and then, as soon as he enters his teens, as a young Communist.

Forbidden games.

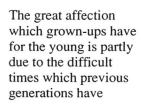

The pioneer's pledge.

*Rural contemplation (left).
The modern thirst (below left).*

Young pioneers' camp in Crimea.

Nobody messes with Comrade Ivan Vassilievitch Koulay, president of the "Red Field" kolkhoz and a representative in the Supreme Soviet of the Byelorussian Republic. His daughter, Professor Maria Ivanovna Romaniuk, is also no intellectual lightweight. However, Sanka Stankevitch, aged thirteen, would prefer a career in the movies. At the art schools, the students are making cautious attempts to liberate themselves from the straitjacket of Socialist Realism. Nevertheless, they are still a long way from regaining the critical spirit of.the years around 1910, when Russian painters and sculptors discovered abstract art.

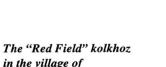

The "Red Field" kolkhoz in the village of Burkovski.

A painter's studio (facing page) in a Siberian art school.

With the advent of glasnost, the streets were soon invaded by a gaudy crowd, decked out in the fetishes of the New Wave. A few hard-rock groups have even dared surreptitiously to sneak words of praise for the anarchist Nestor Makhno into their lyrics. Makhno was a legendary figure in Russia's Civil War, which began after the 1917 Revolution. For lack of anything better, the fans plumb the depths of cheap liquor in their search for signs of a rebellion which does not seem to be happening As for the yuppies, who are not necessarily from apparatchik families, they prefer the "cool" atmosphere of the nightclubs frequented by tourists from the West.

Above: the dance hall in the Hotel Rossiya, Moscow.

Below: a group of teenagers on a seat in the subway.

Below: the Arbat: dreams of freedom and drunkenness.

The "in crowd" after a concert.

Above: at the foot of the steps.

In law, a Russian teenager is responsible for his actions from the age of fourteen. If he has committed a crime, he must stay in prison until his trial. Depending on his sentence, he is then either sent to a juvenile hall, or put on probation somewhere a long way from his own home, where he must register daily at the precinct house. Theoretically, re-education camps allow juvenile delinquents to learn a trade and to continue their studies, but the inmates are frequently made to do manual labor instead. If a juvenile commits a serious felony for which the sentence extends beyond his eighteenth birthday, he is sent on to an adult labor camp on attaining his majority.

Above: visiting day for the family.

Left: the dining hall in an adult labor camp.

Below: a game of chess.

Below: re-education through work.

There are more than five million students in higher education. College students get a scholarship and a room on campus for six years, the longest time permitted in which to graduate. The program for the first two years is the same for every faculty, whatever the chosen specialism. Specialization is only allowed in the junior and senior years. The teaching of Marxism/Leninism is still compulsory, but criticism has been tolerated since Perestroika. Although manual labor is better paid, the country still has countless doctors, lawyers and scientists for whom the material difficulties have been no deterrent to long years of study.

Above: lecture at the Faculty of Medicine, Moscow University.

Right: students learning highway regulations.

Left: Kiev Polytechnic.

The industrial/military complex constitutes a state within a state, and its adherence to Perestroika is questioned by some. The burial of the Warsaw Pact, in February 1991, went unnoticed at a time when international opinion was hypnotized by the Gulf War. From then on, however, those living in Eastern Europe now saw the continued presence of the Red Army as a haunting symbol of the old order. The columns of T70 tanks began to withdraw gradually, and without a fight. Since its defeat in Afghanistan, several republics in the Union itself had anyway begun to doubt the might of the Red Army.

A tank unit near Borissov.

An officer's wedding at the military school in Moghilev.

The RN3 Young Sailors' Club.

An officer takes the oath of allegiance in Moghilev.

Red Army training in Byelorussia.

Alexander Stepanenko, a fashion photographer in Moscow, says: "I hadn't been back to my village for many years. Time seems to have stood still there. It's just the way it was when I was a kid; hay is gathered in before the storm and the old people doze by the window. In the evenings, the youngsters go out into the forest, light a campfire and kick up a rumpus till late at night."

Harvesting in the village of Kissilievsky, in the Moghilev district of Byelorussia.

After work in the fields,
Kissilievsky.

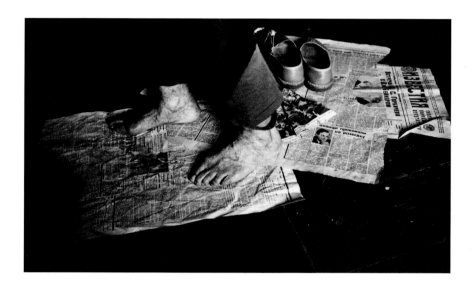

" ... Old Evdokia always leaves her shoes on her doorstep. The Borissov family is celebrating the last day of the sowing season. Grandmother Varvara and Aunt Galina are threshing the wheat while my cousins and Aunt Martinika pose for the photograph. We chatted for so long that we ended up forgetting what we were talking about. The jackdaws have certainly become very daring this year."

There are no more plow-horses in Estonia, but the nuns from Piukhtitiski convent carry on the old traditions and cultivate their fields without the use of artificial fertilizers or pesticides. However, ecological considerations are not what prompts the peasants to store up huge reserves of wood for the winter.

*Facing page top left: Piukhtitiski convent, Estonia; bottom left:
fishermen resting, in the Arkhangelsk region.
Above: marketplace in Nakhodka, near Vladivostok.*

The kolkhoz farms date back to the the collectivization of land in the thirties, while the sovkhoz farms were created under Khrushchev; they employ twenty-six million people. Today, there is serious talk of handing the land back to the peasants, and the abolition of serfdom by Alexander II is sometimes mentioned as a parallel. With the coming of Perestroika, the problems of agriculture are being tackled more openly, as agronomists, economists and sociologists worry over the management of the U.S.S.R.'s fifty-five thousand kolkhozes and sovkhozes.

Above: hay making in the Ukraine. Below: a barn in the Arkhangelsk region.

Right: a couple returning home with a basket of berries.

It is difficult to compare the situation of Russian women with that of women in western countries. In Russia, it is not unusual to see a mother wielding a shovel or driving a giant tractor. In the countryside, the grandmothers, or babushkas, usually continue to share the family home, performing household tasks and helping to educate the children, as well as doing small jobs around the farm. It's a tough life of hard work and frugality, played out against the rigors of the climate, all of which go to explain the women's premature aging. Outside intellectual circles, women still do not have the respect they deserve.

Above: a Black Sea
cruise.

Left: the arrival of
holidaymakers in Odessa.

Below: holidaymakers
line a beach in Yalta, by
the Black Sea.

Officially, 195 million
Soviet citizens, almost
half the population,
take a vacation every
year. Tourists favor the
hotels and holiday
camps on the beaches
of the Black Sea and
the banks of the great
rivers, or the Caucasus
Mountains. Although
standards of comfort in
Russian hotels are still
rather primitive, away
from the seaside
families can enjoy a
largely unspoilt
countryside, where the
joys of wild mushroom
or strawberry picking
have not yet been
supplanted by those of
water sports and theme
parks.

The resort of Massandra.

You won't find everything you need at the Gastronom supermarket: goods on sale include milk, butter, preserves and soft drinks. Fruit and vegetables are black market items! So shopping resembles covering an assault course, and requires great ingenuity and patience. Long lines build up in front of the baker's stall, and people wait for hours to buy a pair of stockings or a hunk of

Above: the Gastronom supermarket in Moscow. Right: standing in line at a clothes store. Far right: a lucrative trade in French sticks.

sausage. It takes almost a whole afternoon before you can even cross the threshold of MacDonald's in Pushkin Square, with its illusion of crossing into the west. An alternative street trade in bric-a-brac, art, and handcrafted items is also carried on, and a jumble of stalls block the sidewalks, especially in the Arbat, giving Moscow the cheerful, jokey, busy look of a huge flea market.

Far left: flea-market trader in Sokolniki Park, Moscow. Left: MacDonald's, Pushkin Square, Moscow.

The elaborate ceremonies of the ZAK wedding bureau, and the pomp and circumstance of the Party are no longer in favor with young couples, who now prefer a religious marriage ceremony. However, couples do still gather before the Tomb of the Unknown Soldier at the foot of the Kremlin to lay a wreath of flowers. Russians marry young, generally before the age of twenty-five; and divorce is very quick.

Below: a young married couple in front of the Lenin Mausoleum. Below left: taking the air in the local park.

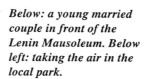

Right: a park bench in Moscow.

Above: a couple receiving a religious blessing of their marriage; the civil ceremony comes first.
Left: a wedding car, Armenia.

Left: a modern couple contemplate reminders of a more formal age.

Scenes of everyday life: gypsies in Moldavia.

Chekhov, Tolstoy and Pushkin wrote unforgettable passages about the life and customs of the gypsies, particularly the "Dimilié Witche" who were the czars' appointed musicians. Their numbers were cruelly decimated by the Germans during World War II, and they now earn a precarious living as blacksmiths, tinkers and fortune-tellers. A few of the lucky ones perform at the Romene Theater, but they have lost all their spontaneity. Far from being integrated into society, gypsies lead a wandering life, trying to escape the net of the authorities, who give them a hard time, and keep them on the bread line. Deeply religious, the gypsies have also retained their superstitions: these two boys, for instance, will not be allowed to have their hair cut until their wedding day, in accordance with a vow made by their parents

after a miraculous cure. Not all the gypsy tribes speak the same language, and they still maintain a caste system, a vestige of their origins on the Indian subcontinent.

The Russian Orthodox Church, which celebrated its millenium in 1988, remains the largest Slavic religious community. It is run by the Holy Synod, the Patriarch of Moscow and All the Russias. Persecuted under communism, despite the reestablishment by Stalin of both an official church and the partriachy of Moscow during the Second World War, it has been slowly rediscovering its freedom of expression since the mid-1980s. Today, the faithful flock to the services held in places of worship once called "museums of atheism" and which have now rediscovered their original purpose. Orthodox priests wear heavy chasubles encrusted with sparkling stones; the church walls, covered with icons and frescoes, echo to the solemn and poignant sounds of polyphonic chants, some specifically devised by the most talented of Russia's composers, including Rachmaninoff and Tchaikovsky.

Below: morning prayer in Uniate church, Ukraine.

Above: a nighttime procession, Pecherski monastery in Kiev.

The celebration of Easter remains the most important religious festival of the Orthodox Church. On this occasion, the faithful bring specially prepared Easter dishes to be blessed by the priests: kulitch, a sweetened yeast-bread flavored with oriental spices; colored eggs decorated with traditional designs; and the paskha, a dessert made from cream cheese, butter and cream in a pyramid-shaped mold. After the mass and the congratulatory kiss, the congregation goes home to feast after forty days of Lenten abstention.

Left: kulitch and painted eggs.

Left: believers crowd in front of a church in Moscow. Below left: the feast of Mary, Mother of God.

Below: Orthodox priests process along a route strewn with flowers, blessing the crowds as they go.

Facing page: religious ceremony, Zagorsk.

A funeral in Uzbek.

Prayer in the streets of Samarkand.

The faithful in a mosque.

Moscow is not unmoved by the high birthrate in a central Asia dominated by Islam. Muslims now constitute almost a quarter of the total population of the U.S.S.R. Most of these are Sunni Muslims, who live in Kazakh, and in the Urals and Siberia, and who share the Caucasus with the Shi'ite Muslims. There are also powerful communities of Ismaili Muslims in Pamir. The Koran is taught mainly at the Miri-Arab University in Bukhara, and at the Islamic Institute in Tashkent.

When the government of Lithuania handed back the keys of Vilnius cathedral to the religious authorities in 1988, the priests of the largest Roman Catholic community in the U.S.S.R. rushed to unearth their old cassocks, dating from before Vatican II, from the cupboards. The past now had a future.

Above: a mass in Vilnius cathedral.

Left: Lithuanian bishops.

The Armenians were converted to Christianity by Gregory the Illuminator in AD 301. The Armenian/ Gregorian dogma soon split from the Church of Constantinople by recognizing the Monophysitic doctrine. This doctrine, which admits the existence of only one aspect of Christ, was condemned by the Council of Chalcedon in AD 451. The head of the Armenian church, the Catholicos, lives in Echmiadzin, northeast of the Armenian capital city of Erevan.

Above: the Catholicos officiating at a service Church of Echmiadzin.

Facing page: Armenian priests in ceremonial robes.

Officially, there are still more than 1,800,000 Jews living in the Soviet Union, despite massive emigration to Israel and the United States. Although the synagogues have been able officially to reopen their doors, the Jewish religion continues to be misunderstood by some Russians, who are still guilty of distrusting those whom they have persecuted for so long.

The Moscow synagogue is situated down a little alley in the Leportovo district.

The lamas of the
Gelug-pa movement,
which has adopted a
doctrine resembling the
Tibetan Buddhist
dogma, have enormous
prestige in the
republics of Tuva and
Kalmyk, and in the
regions of Chita and
Irkutsk.

*This page: religious
objects in a Buriatic
temple.*

*Facing page: a Buddhist
dignitary and his acolytes.*

Villages in northern and central Russia.

A Ukrainian wheatfield in summer.

From the frontiers of the Ukraine and Finland as far as the Pacific Ocean stretches a vast territory which man has never really been able to control. The climate is a harsh one: a hot, dry summer follows an all too short spring. Autumn is rainy and misty, and throughout the winter blizzards whistle across the plains of central Russia.

Temperatures fall to
-40°C, and may drop as
low as -70°C in
Siberia. Great rivers
cross the interminable
forests. Central Russia
is an impoverished
land, where only the
birch flourishes. Its
bark is used to make
lapti, traditional
peasant shoes.

The sun setting over a reed-bed.

The patterns created by trunks and branches illustrate two aspects of the Russian forest.

*The slender trunks of
silver birch trees stand
tall and straight in a
forest near Moscow.*

After the storm ...

Above: an island defines the break between lowering sky and sunset-tinged water. Above left: a river flows into the salt waters of the Sea of Okhotsk.

Dramatic skies over the western side of the Kamchatka Peninsula.

The Ukraine, "the
granary of Europe,"
was swept first by the
Mongolian hordes in
the thirteenth century,
then in modern times
by the conquering,
expansionist armies of
the western powers.
The Ukraine is also the
homeland of the
Zaporogski Cossacks.

In a natural reserve, situated on the borders of the Ukraine with Byelorussia and Poland, a herd of the last bison in Europe (above) roam.

Left: a herd of the same tough breed of ponies as were ridden by the Mongol invaders in the thirteenth century.

The Volga rises in the foothills of the Valdai Hills, 300 kilometres west of Moscow, and reaches the Caspian Sea after a journey of over 2,000 miles. The river has been used since the ninth century for transporting goods between northern Europe and central Asia. It flows through the cities of Kalinin, Gorkiy, Kazan and Volgograd before finishing its course in the great estuary at Astrakhan, and pouring its millions of gallons of fresh water into the rapidly draining Caspian Sea, whose waters are the very distillation of civilization. The sturgeon now avoid the seaboard, and unload their precious cargo of caviar elsewhere.

The unbroken banks of a slow-flowing river.

In its upper reaches, the Volga flows through various Central Russian towns.

*In winter, drifting ice
hinders the river's flow.*

*Flamingos on the
Caspian Sea.*

The Lena flows from
Lake Baykal northward
into the Arctic Ocean:
a journey of more than
2,500 miles. Its course
is restricted and
serpentine as far as
Yakutsk, then the Lena
straightens out
majestically as it
crosses the desolate
Tundra. At its mouth
the Lena has formed a
huge delta, where its
innumberable branches
are lost in the sediment
deposited by its waters.

The Lena's banks, which are sometimes over three miles apart, shelter the fossilized remains of countless prehistoric animals, including mounds of mammoth bones that are pillaged by ivory traffickers.

On its right bank, the
Lena cuts into the ancient
Verkhoyansk Range.

The river is sufficiently
calm for freighters to
navigate as far as
Yakutsk.

The region around the great River Amur, and where it flows into the salty waters of the Sea of Okhotsk, is a barren land of mosses and lichens, where climatic conditions stunt the growth of the trees. Nevertheless, it is an area rich in game, and the stunted trees do give way to thick forests and the taiga.

The taiga around the Gulf of Anadyr.

At almost 375 miles long, Lake Baykal, situated close to the Mongolian border, is Siberia's largest expanse of fresh water. The lake extends in a crescent-moon shape along the spur of the Barguzin Mountains, where fur-trapping contrasts sharply with the heavy industry based around the mining centers of Irkutsk, Angorsk and Ulan Ude to the south. The waste from their factories flows into the lake, contributing both to the water's rise in temperature and to its pollution. This in turn disturbs the lake's ecosystem, which supports unique flora and fauna. The lake's subsoil also contains great geological and paleontological riches, making the area a most important scientific site.

The tops of the Barguzin Mountains.

*The vast Siberian forest
meets the clear waters of
Lake Baykal.*

The Chukchi Peninsula at the easternmost tip of Siberia is covered in summer with a sparse vegetation of lichens and dwarf trees. More than 20,000 years ago, an obscure race from the Mongolian steppes made the long journey to the Peninsula, and crossed over the icebound Bering Straits. That race became known as the Native Americans.

Next stop: Alaska.

A barren landscape at the edge of the world.

Above: hillside geysers.

Right: an eruption on Mount Tolbatchinski.

Below: Klyuchevskaya, the highest active volcano in Europe and Asia.

In 1648, just over 150 years after Christopher Columbus discovered America, the first conquerors of this distant and inhospitable region faced the fantastic spectacle of the great chaos at the origin of the Earth. The peninsula is shaken at regular intervals by twenty-eight active volcanos, of which Klyuchevskaya is one of the world's highest. Klyuchevskaya's snowcapped peak thrusts upward to a height of more than 14,000 feet above the incandescent lava flows, the crackling gray cinders and the innumerable, thunderous geysers.

The substratum of this apocalyptic landscape contains huge reserves of gold, oil and coal. The majority of the population has taken refuge on the banks of the Sea of Okhotsk and lives by breeding reindeer, and crab fishing. In the mountains of the Kamchatka Peninsula, the tracks of brown bears and Siberian tigers can still be seen.

Rare Siberian tigers come down to drink at pools such as these.

The highest points of the Kamchatka Peninsula reach over 12,000 feet.

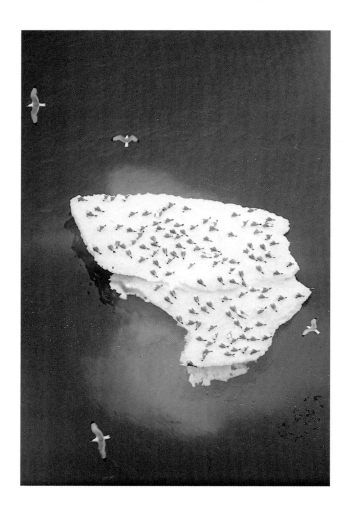

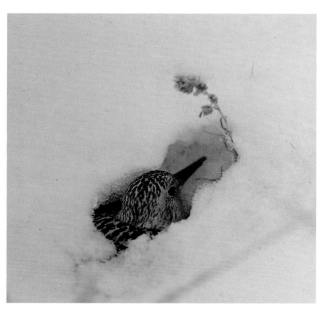

Top: flying over an ice floe.

A sudden, severe snow storm caught this nesting bird unawares.

It was Thomas Corvin's American sailors who, in 1881, first landed on Wrangel Island in the extreme north of Siberia. The winters are freezing, and the polar night lasts from November to January. Yet around fifty species of birds nest there all year round, and many others migrate there during the summer to raise their young. Wrangel Island constitutes a natural reserve that shelters some hundred thousand white geese, driven to the area from the polluted estuaries of the Lena and Kolyma rivers.

Every year, large colonies of eider ducks come to seek refuge on Wrangel Island.

The sparse vegetation that covers Wrangel Island supports various migrating birds, among them the Arctic Tern, the Red Phalarope, and the Rough-legged Hawk.

A few family groups of polar bears can be seen on the Island's snowy slopes. The she-bear hollows out a shelter in the ice, and when it has been sufficiently warmed up, she gives birth to a blind and hairless cub. Before leaving terra firma for the ice field, the bear cub, who is still dependent on its mother, learns the first rudiments of hunting. Scientists on Wrangel Island are now closely observing the habits of these polar bears.

Above: en route for the ice field.

Top and facing page: the entrance to a bear's den, hollowed out of the ice.

Researchers on Wrangel Island follow the wanderings of the walrus colonies very closely. Walruses haul themselves onto the drifting ice floes using their upper canines, which can grow to over three feet in some males; these teeth are also used to extract food from the sea's depths. An adult walrus can weigh more than a ton, and can grow up to sixteen feet in length. For the inhabitants of the Arctic, the walrus provides meat, fat, leather, and ivory.

A walrus colony gathered on the drifting ice.

A lake on Wrangel Island, during the short Arctic summer.

During the Arctic summer, colorful flowers push their way through the melting snow.

Situated southwest of the Bering Strait, the Commander Islands were discovered in 1741 by the Danish explorer, Vitus Bering, known as Commander. Several species of animals take refuge on the Islands, and are the subject of an important program of scientific research.

Close-up of a seal.

A herd of reindeer roam the treeless landscape.

Seals sunbathing.

Researchers' bivouac.

The Kurile
Archipelago stretches
for more than 625
miles between Cape
Lopatka, at the
southern tip of the
Kamchatka Peninsula,
to the island of
Hokkaido. The
Japanese have long
demanded that the
southernmost islands in
the archipelago be
restored to them – they
were confiscated at the
end of World War II.

*Basalt cliffs, looking like
massive organ pipes,
plunge into the Sea of
Okhotsk.*

More than three quarters of Kirghiz lies in the Pamirs and the Tian Shan Mountains which straddle the Chinese frontier. These northernmost peaks of the Himalayan range rise to a height of more than 21,000 feet. Down their steep slopes tumble glaciers, waterfalls and torrential streams at which the last of the snow tigers come to

drink. The slopes do support vegetation, including rare and precious medicinal plants, walnut trees, hemp, and vines. Barley also grows up to altitudes of 10,000 feet.

Top left: a mountain lake on Sary-Chelek, Kirghiz.
Top right: mountain meadows in Djety-Ogouz.

Above: the snowy foothills of the Pamirs.

Left: the Lenin Peak, 22,000 feet high.

By the shores of the Caspian Sea, along the frontier with Iran and Afghanistan, lies the land of the Turkmen horsemen, who still hunt with falcons. In a landscape eroded by salt water – a quart of water from the lakes of Yorolanduz contains around ten ounces of salt – there are sometimes carpets of poppies to delight the eye.

A salt-saturated river in the Yorolanduz region.

A field of wild poppies.

The overlapping enclaves of Kabardin-Balkar, Chechen-Ingush and Ossetian typify the ethnic mosaic of the Caucasus Mountains, which form the true demarcation line between East and West. The virgin slopes of the Elbrus and the Kazbek peaks, which top 15,000 feet, are becoming a mecca for climbers and skiers the world over, and are gradually developing resort facilities. The lower slopes shelter the vineyards that produce the famous Caucasian wines.

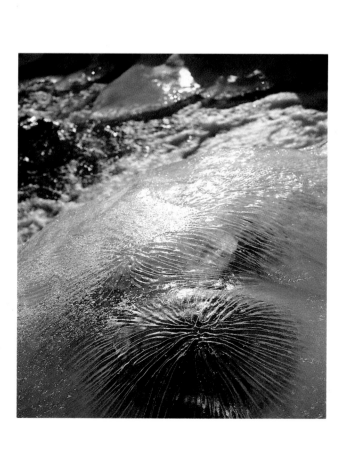

A ski-lift close to the summit of Mount Dongov-Orun is dwarfed by the majesty of the mountains themselves.

The drying up of the Aral Sea vies with the nuclear accident at Chernobyl as one of the greatest ecological disasters of the twentieth century. During the 1960s, an irrigation project was launched which deflected the waters of the Aral Sea's two feeder rivers away into the sands of Kazakh. In thirty years, the shores of the Aral Sea receded by around 125 miles, leaving whole fleets of fishing boats high and dry. The Kazakhs are still asking themselves which cruel, modern god deprived them of their sea.

Wrecked and stranded fishing boats near the former port of Muynak.

The despair of a Kazakh fisherman.

TOWNS

The Cathedral of St. Basil the Blessed, Moscow.

The statue of Minin and Pozharsky, in front of the Cathedral of St. Basil the Blessed.

The Yelokhinski Church: portal in "Russian Empire" style.

In the Exhibition of Economic Achievements stands the Friendship of Peoples Fountain, each gilded bronze statue representing a republic.

In the course of the last few decades, the megalopolis of Moscow has continued to expand, swallowing up suburbs and neighboring villages. These have been replaced by interminable blocks of concrete, interspersed with a multitude of industrial complexes. A few old wooden houses still stand in the southwest, survivors of the fires that once ravaged the city several times a century. The center of Moscow is reached along wide avenues where neoclassical edifices, vestiges of the Stalinist period, vie for position with modern buildings, government offices and other contemporary structures. The disparate and often heavy architecture of the capital does not discourage more and more tourists from flocking to Moscow every year.

The Space Obelisk, built in 1964 to celebrate Russian successes in the field of space flight.

The Cosmos Hotel, a luxury hotel built by the French in the sixties.

The tall spire of the Ukraina Hotel, built in 1956.

The entrance to the Tretyakov Gallery.

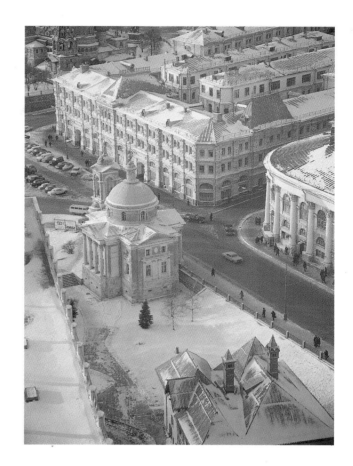

In the years prior to Perestroika, opponents of the regime - Ginsburg, Sakharov, his wife Helena Bonner, and many more - came to speak to the public at the foot of Pushkin's statue in a little square situated away from the main streets.

Top right: Church of Saint Anne's Conception. Above right: snow decorates a city tree. Right: statue of the writer Nikolai Gogol.

Left: the embankment of the River Moskva.

Kreml is the Russian word for "fortress." The Kremlin was built between 1485 and 1508, in the reign of Ivan III, by Italian architects who were inspired by the defenses of the Sforzas' castle near Milan. Originally, the high, thick walls were to protect the czars and the boyars against invasions. A moat was also dug around the fortress, but was later filled in. Cradle of the Russian empire, the Kremlin contains a multitude of palaces and churches whose onion-shaped domes pierce the skies.

One onion-shaped dome of the Church of the Deposition of the Robe, attached to the Kremlin's Terem Palace.

The gilded domes of the churches around Cathedral Square in the Kremlin.

A nighttime view of the Kremlin, with the Cathedral of St. Basil the Blessed in the right foreground.

Ivan the Terrible, Boris Godunov, Feodor II - the Kremlin's walls shelter memories of all the most troubled and disturbed periods of Russian history. Then, in 1613, the boyar Mikhail Romanov was crowned czar, thereby founding a long and famous dynasty, and bringing some stability to the country.

Top: inside the Cathedral of the Assumption.

Above: the interior of the Palace of Facets, part of the Great Kremlin Palace.

Colored illustration from the Book of the Coronation of Mikhail Romanov.

View over Cathedral Square.

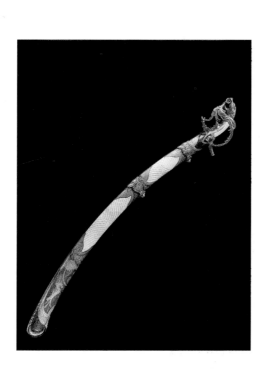

Inside the Palace of Facets.

In Cathedral Square, the facades of the palaces, decorated by Italian artists, contrast strongly with the outward sobriety of the ancient, golden-domed churches. Inside, however, these contain all the treasures of a religious hierarchy enriched by several generations of reigning monarchs. Cathedral Square is a sumptuous architectural feast which includes the Church of the Deposition of the Robe, the Cathedral of the Assumption, the Palace of Facets and the Cathedral of the Annunciation, where the royal family were baptized.

The walls of Moscow's palaces and churches are covered in frescoes recounting Russia's history.

An open-air swimming pool was built on the site of the ancient Cathedral of the Saviour, destroyed after the Revolution.

Trumpet solo in front of the Space Obelisk.

Below: free-form skating.
Below right: eyes down —
a swimmer has just dived
beneath the ice on the
Moskva River.

There are almost twelve million people living in Moscow, not counting visitors, who number nearly as many again. In winter, Muscovites take advantage of the extensive parks and of the great avenues that cut across the city to do all sorts of sports, from cross-country skiing to ice skating. There are even those who are brave enough to swim in the open-air pools.

A representation of the Virgin and Child which is typical of a pictorial art strongly influenced by the Italian Renaissance.

Founded around 1010 by Yaroslav the Wise, Prince of Kiev and Novgorod, the town of Yaroslavl lies on the road to Arkhangelsk, the largest port on the White Sea and Russia's only outlet to the sea in the sixteenth century. Destroyed by the Tatars in 1238, Yaroslavl was annexed by Moscow in 1471. The churches of Nikola Nadein, St. John the Baptist, and Elijah the Prophet are examples of a particular architectural style in which the onion-shaped domes are linked with pyramid-shaped bell towers.

The Church of St. John the Baptist.

The Church of Elijah the Prophet.

The Church of Nikola Nadein.

Rostov the Great is the former residence of the Metropolitans, and was founded in the ninth century. It contains a number of religious sites, including the five-cupola Cathedral of the Assumption whose bell tower contains a bell that weighs thirty-two metric tons, and can be heard for twelve miles around.

Above: the Cathedral of the Assumption.

Facing page: inside the Church of the Saviour.

Right: the descent from the cross as depicted on a sixteenth-century tapestry.

Below: Rostov's kremlin seen from Lake Nero.

St. Sergius of Radonezh was a thirteenth-century hermit so solitary he shared his meals with a bear. A small community eventually formed around him, spreading the gospel right up to the shores of the distant White Sea, and exhorting the peasants to revolt against Tatar oppression. The monastery was destroyed in the fifteenth century, and the occupants dispersed, but the body of the saint was found to be miraculously intact. A new monastery, protected by fortified walls, survived two Polish attacks, in 1609 and 1618. The little town of Sergiyev thus became a site of pilgrimage and the symbol of Russian patriotism. The town was renamed Zagorsk in 1919. It houses the austere Trinity Cathedral, decorated by the famous medieval ikon painter Andrey Rublyov, and the astonishing Cathedral of the Assumption.

The golden dome of the Cathedral of the Assumption is central to this view of Zagorsk. To the left is the four-storied bell tower designed by the Italian architect, Rastrelli. Further left still stands the Refectory where the election of the Patriarch of Moscow took place.

Above right: the Refectory. Right: a tapestry depicting the story of St. Sergius.

The wars between the city of Prince Vladimir Monomakh, built in AD 116, and its rival, Suzdal, bear witness to the many fierce battles between Russian cities throughout the medieval period. Vladimir emerged the winner from this conflict, but the principality of Vladimir-Suzdal was first destroyed by the Tatars in 1238, and then fell under the rule of Moscow in the fifteenth century. The Cathedral of the Assumption dominates the plain of the Klyazma River; it is a masterpiece of sacred art that was copied by the Italian architect Fioravanti within Moscow's Kremlin.

Domes and tympanums.

The twelfth-century Cathedral of the Assumption.

Fresco of Mary, Mother of God, Cathedral of the Dormition.

St. George's bell tower, Cathedral of the Assumption.

Right: decorative details, and (far right) wooden sculpture, Cathedral of St. George.

In defiance of fires, epidemics, and invasions by both the Tatars and the Poles, the inhabitants of Suzdal, about 130 miles from Moscow, built many churches and monasteries, whose towers, spires, and onion-shaped domes dominate the city's skyline. They also founded a school of icon painting, and encouraged artists and sculptors in wood. In an open-air museum have been gathered together the finely carved wooden churches that the city's carpenters built in the surrounding villages.

Right: wooden churches in the Museum of Rural Architecture.

Left: the Savior Monastery of St. Euthymius.

The Smolny Institute, a former finishing school for young ladies founded by Catherine II in the Age of Enlightenment, became the headquarters of Lenin and Trotsky during the October Revolution. Today, the buildings are occupied by Party officials.

The Narva Triumphal Arch (above) commemorates the victories of the Russian armies over the forces of Charles XII (1704) and Napoleon (1812), under the emperors Peter the Great and Alexander I respectively.

Leningrad began simply as a few houses clustered beneath the ramparts of a fortress built to defend territories captured from the Swedes by Peter the Great, who named the new city St. Petersburg. Eager to open up his country to the influence of a Europe at the height of her powers, the Emperor called on the services of western architects to construct an entire capital city that would be worthy of his ambitions. After the October

Polar night over the Neva River, seen from the roof of the Hermitage.

Revolution, the new leaders moved their political infrastructure to Moscow, and the former capital was renamed Leningrad. Besieged by the Germans during World War II, the inhabitants held out for 900 days against famine, and the bombardments of enemy artillery.

A colored engraving of the banks of the Neva River in the time of Catherine II.

St. Petersburg was a rapidly expanding port in the eighteenth century.

The doorway to Peter the Great's palace.

The Marly Pavilion.

The park surrounding Peter the Great's palace was designed by Leblond, a pupil of André Lenôtre, Louis XIV's gardener. Water flows through the park via a series of steps, basins, and fountains, before pouring into the Gulf of Finland.

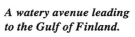

A watery avenue leading to the Gulf of Finland.

The Samson fountain.

Left: the Chesma Church.

Above: the Bridge of Kisses.

Below: in the background, the entrance to the Admiralty buildings.

The European influence on traditional Russian architecture has produced some curious hybrids, such as the pinnacled Chesma Church built in the shape of a Latin cross, and the portal of the Peter-Paul Fortress, guarded by the statues of Reason in Affairs of State and of the Goddess of War. However, the columns of the Admiralty buildings on the banks of the Neva River, and the Bridge of Kisses are reminiscent of pure Dutch and Venetian styles.

One of the two columns of the Admiralty buildings.

The great hall of the Mikhail Palace.

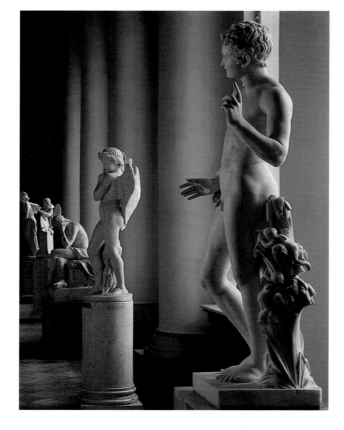

The unreliable banks of the River Neva and the marshes that flooded the area were stabilized and drained at an immense cost in human lives. Canals were dug, and numerous palaces were built for the royal family. The Italian architect Carlo Rossi drew up the plans for the palace of the Grand Duke Michael, brother of Alexander I. Guarded by imposing stone lions, it has housed the Russian Museum, and an important collection of contemporary art since 1898.

The Bank Bridge over the Griboyedova Canal, guarded by four griffons with gilded wings.

The Winter Palace.

The spire of the Admiralty buildings.

The five palaces of the State Hermitage contain more than two million masterpieces, including twenty-five paintings by Rembrandt and works by Gainsborough, Leonardo da Vinci, Raphael, Michelangelo, Titian, Murillo, and Velasquez. An impressive collection of Impressionist works alone fills forty-seven rooms, and includes paintings by Monet, Sisley, Pissarro, Renoir, Gauguin, and Cézanne. The Winter Palace, in which Peter the Great died, and which was the residence of the czars until the Revolution, was remodeled many times, the final version being a baroque edifice embellished with malachite urns and Carrara marble staircases.

Reception room.

Portrait gallery of the heroes of the 1812 Campaign.

The Jourdain Staircase.

The Kirov Theater, formerly known as the Mariya Theater.

Dance, through which the Russian "spiritual flight" (Pushkin) is expressed, was fixed as classical ballet. The patrons of the Mariya Theater (1860), which became the Academy Theater of the Kirov Ballet, flocked to see the greatest ballerinas and dancers in Europe. Pavlova and Nijinsky were just two of the outstanding graduates of this national school run by Russian choreographers who both exported their unique style, and also, in the early twentieth century, collaborated on productions with foreign artists such as Cocteau and Picasso. Nureyev, Vassiliev, Plissetskaya, and Ulanova would eventually perform before an even wider public, while Prokofiev, like Stravinsky at the beginning of the century, helped to create, via his music, an atmosphere and style that came to characterize Russian ballet.

Sunbathing at the foot of the Peter-Paul Fortress.

Chess: a national pastime, played with enthusiasm and concentration whatever the weather.

Eighteenth- and nineteenth-century portraits of some of Kostroma's upper-middle-class citizens.

Kostroma, situated about 200 miles northeast of Moscow at the confluence of the Volga and Kostroma rivers, was founded in the twelfth century. Later, its profitable timber and linen industries, much in demand at the time, enabled the city fathers to build a city largely in the finest classical imperial style, although the cathedrals attached to the Ipatiev and Apparition of God monasteries are splendid examples of sixteenth- and seventeenth-century architecture.

The River Kostroma and Ipatiev Monastery.

Important archeological evidence has recently been unearthed, in the form of inscriptions on wooden logs, proving that, while Western Europe was still in the Dark Ages, Novgorod was a progressive city. An independent city-state between 1136 and 1478, Novgorod was an important commercial crossroads in trade with the Hanseatic League. For many Russians, Novgorod remains a symbol of resistance to Western invasion; at the edge of Lake Peipus, in the thirteenth century, Alexander Nevsky and the city's defenders put to flight the army of the Teutonic Knights.

The icon is a tradition, dating from the eleventh century, that originated in Constantinople. The Orthodox church throughout the world still practices the subtle and demanding art of painting murals and illuminating wood panels with religious portraits. Although icons generally represent scenes from the Gospels, they occasionally relate episodes from Russian history. Left: icon illustrating a scene from the twelfth-century war between the city-states of Novgorod and Suzdal.

The city of Pskov, situated on the Velikaya River about 160 miles southwest of Leningrad, played an active part in the fight against both the Teutonic Knights and the Lithuanian princes, before being forced to bow to the supremacy of Moscow in 1510. It was in Pskov that Czar Nicholas II abdicated in 1917. One notable historic building to survive second world war damage is the seventeenth-century, limestone Cathedral of the Trinity, built in a series of crossed vaults.

The sixteenth-century church of St. Isidore.

The Pskov kremlin dominates the plain of the Velikaya River.

The cradle of Russian civilization in the Middle Ages, modern Kiev is one of Europe's major urban centers. Capital of the Ukraine, it is still a city of green spaces where many churches and monasteries bear witness to the conversion to Christianity of its ruler, Grand Prince Vladimir, in AD 988. Between the tenth and twelfth centuries, Kiev's influence extended as far as Central Europe. Standing at the crossroads of two great civilizations, the Slav and the Byzantine, Kiev is proud of its magnificent Cathedral of St. Sophia, erected by Byzantine architects in the early eleventh century. The design is based on that of St. Sophia in Constantinople.

Top: the central cupola of the Cathedral of St. Sophia. Above: a mosaic of the Praying Virgin, protectress of Russia.

Many of Kiev's churches and monasteries (right) are still surrounded by parkland. The Dnepr River can be seen in the distance.

Virtually razed to the ground by the Tatars in the early thirteenth century, Kiev also suffered Lithuanian and Polish invasions up to the eighteenth century. In 1774, Kiev and the Ukraine, most of whose inhabitants are Christian Orthodox, once again became Russian, under the impetus of Bohdan Khmelnytsky. Between 1941 and 1943 Kiev was at the center of the fierce battles for which it was honored as one of the few "martyr cities."

*The Golden Gate, built in
the eleventh century and
situated near the
Cathedral of St. Sophia.*

Sevastopol, once a Tatar city, fiercely resisted the massed attack of the Anglo-French forces that disembarked on the shores of Crimea in 1854. When he took the city after a year-long siege, Napoleon III ended Czar Nicholas I's claim to control of the sea passage through the Dardanelles. Traditionally devoted to naval, military, and civilian construction, Sevastopol is also a center for the study of the marine biology of the southern seas.

Above: the ruins of ancient Chersonesus, founded in 421 BC.

Below: the Siege of Sevastopol, 1854. Left: a monument to lost ships. Far left: the second Siege of Sevastopol, July 1942.

**A bridge over the Western
Dvina links the old and
the new city.**

Riga, the capital of Latvia, was founded in the thirteenth century at the mouth of the Western Dvina River by the Teutonic Knights. It is a very Western city that still bears traces of its cosmopolitan past, having been occupied successively by the Poles, the Swedes, and the Russians, before being annexed to the Soviet Union in 1944. The conditions of that annexation are today the subject of great controversy. The old city is a mixture of the architectural styles of its successive inhabitants – from Gothic vaulting to oppressive Stalinist constructions.

Stained-glass windows in Riga's Doma Cathedral.

Vilnius, capital of Lithuania, extends over a series of natural terraces at the confluence of the Neris and Vilnia rivers, about 190 miles from the Baltic Sea. The city possesses one of the oldest universities in Europe, and, in the early sixteenth century, began printing books in the Lithuanian language. Since 1560, however, Lithuania has experienced only a few years of independence, passing successively into the hands of the Poles, the Swedes, the Germans, and finally the Russians.

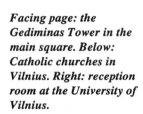

Facing page: the Gediminas Tower in the main square. Below: Catholic churches in Vilnius. Right: reception room at the University of Vilnius.

Founded more than three thousand years before Christ, Samarkand was an important staging post on the caravan route to Asia. It was conquered by Alexander the Great's army in 329 BC, and by Genghis Khan's hordes in 1220. Tamerlane (Timur the lame) rebuilt, enlarged, and embellished the city in 1369.

Below: the Gur-e Amir Mausoleum.

Left: the cupola of the Amir Mausoleum.

Above: Reghistan Square: the fifteenth-century Ulugh-Beg Madaris (religious academy), and the seventeenth-century Chir-dor Madaris, and Tillia-Kari Madaris.

"The pearl of the Orient" is adorned with gardens, palaces, and mosques, of which one of the most spectacular is the octagonal mausoleum of Gur-e Amir, with its ivory-inlaid doors. Tamerlaine is buried deep in the crypt, in a green marble tomb.

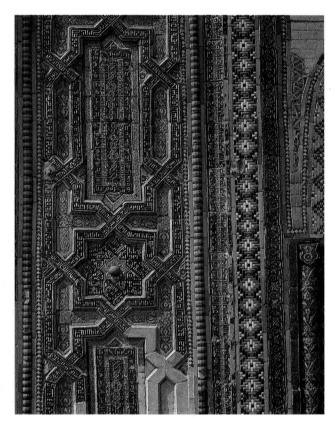

The dome of the Gur-e Amir Mausoleum and details from the fifteenth-century seraglio of Ak, a reminder of Uzbek civilization.

The name Bukhara is derived from the Sanskrit word *vikara*, meaning monastery. An Arab city from the eighth century, it was the capital of the Samanids in the ninth and tenth centuries. The city was built in the delta of the Zeravshan River, and many monuments testify to its former position as an important cultural, artistic, and commercial center. Attracted by this wealth, the Russians subjugated the region in 1868.

Char-Minar Mosque (1807). Interior of the Chashma Leons Mausoleum (fourteenth and fifteenth centuries).

The twelfth-century Kalyan Minaret. Southern facade of the ninth/tenth-century Samani Mausoleum.

The Kalyan Mosque, built between the twelfth and sixteenth centuries.

REPUBLICS

An Azeri, aged 130.

Mongolian girl from the Upper Altay region.

The villagers' meals are always accompanied with tea.

The well is the villagers' only source of water.

Fishermen returning home after a day's work on Lake Latcha.

The village of Kargopol.

*Below: fifteenth-century
icon of Saint Blaise,
Petrozavodsk Museum.*

*Above: hunting scene
from an icon. Right:
detail of the construction
of an isba. Far right:
close-up of a wood-
shingled roof.*

The Kiji Islands, situated at the northern edge of the vast Lake Ladoga, and very near Leningrad, were an important staging post for the merchants of Novgorod on their way to the ports of the Hanseatic League. Most of their isbas were destroyed by fire, but some striking constructions can still be seen, all built without nails or pegs, using techniques which are now forgotten.

Fourteenth-century church of the Resurrection of St. Lazarus, transported from Murmansk.

Tallinn: the spire of Saint-Olaf's Church dominates the medieval town center.

A torchlight procession passes the University.

Estonia is the smallest and least populated of the Baltic states. The capital, Tallinn, was a Danish fortress before it was sold to the Teutonic Order in the fourteenth century. Estonia was subjugated by the Swedes in 1564, and then conquered by Peter the Great after his victory over the armies of Charles XII in 1721. Although one third of Tallinn's inhabitants are now of Russian extraction, the city has great respect for its ancient heritage, and enjoys staging traditional events.

Traditional dress of the Guild of Chimney Sweeps.

Medieval doorway of the Guild of the Black Heads.

Tallinn, capital of Estonia, is a former Hanseatic League port.

Traditional dress of the inhabitants of the island of Saaremaa.

Sunset gilds a group of stacks, neatly set out behind a typical, one-storied farmhouse.

Remains of the eleventh-century Castle of Trakai.

After uniting with Poland, the Lithuanians occupied Byelorussia and their armies marched as far as Moscow, to occupy a throne which had been left vacant by the disappearance of Boris Godunov, and the quarrels between the boyars. In 1795, following the partition of Poland, Lithuania was annexed to the Russian empire. If the Lithuanians are granted autonomy, they will probably become the link between Western Europe and the various Soviet republics.

The little village of Messedess; the boulders were deposited by glaciers during the Quaternary Period.

A sixteenth-century dwelling in Kaunas, Lithuania's second city.

The town hall in Kaunas.

Trout farming on the Black River.

The port of Poti is on the same latitude as Rome.

The homeland of the former seminarian Joseph Stalin was converted to Christianity in the fifth century. Georgia placed itself under the aegis of orthodox Russia in 1793 to protect itself from Turkish expansionism. Bordered by the Black Sea, it is a region of eternally snow-capped mountains, dense forests, and fertile valleys that produce almost all the U.S.S.R.'s citrus fruits and tea. Tbilisi, on the Kura River, was an important stage on the caravan route from Persia. The Russians dubbed it "the Florence of the Caucasus."

The village of Chatily, in the region of Khievsureti ("land of the dawn").

Tbilisi, "the Florence of the Caucasus."

This hurdy-gurdy player and his driver are on their way to a village wedding.

An Abkhazian wearing the traditional cherkeska.

Protecting lemon trees from frost.

An Abkhazian landscape.

*An Abkhazian woman
holding a treasured
souvenir of her youth.*

*A Svan musician with a
harp he has crafted
himself.*

Following the wars against the Persians and the Ottomans, between 1804 and 1828, the eastern part of Christian Armenia was absorbed into the Russian empire. The Erzurum region remained under Turkish rule, however, and more than two million Armenians were exterminated by the Turks during World War I. Many of the survivors scattered throughout the world, as far afield as the United States and Canada. These scattered Armenians have always had a strong sense of unity, showing great sympathy for those left behind, and doing much to help the victims of the 1988 earthquake.

Right: in the shade of a wild vine.

Below: gathered for a drink.

Young married couple,
Leninakan

Yerevan, the capital of
Armenia, situated at the
foot of Mount Ararat.

Yerevan, the capital of Armenia, was founded in the ninth century BC, and is situated overlooking the deep valley of the River Razdan. Its pink tufa and black basalt buildings are built no higher than four stories, for fear of earthquakes, and they give an impression of sturdy strength. The basilicas are built in the form of a Greek cross with several apses, each topped by a conical tower or a stone cupola above a circular or polygonal tympanum. The plain walls and carved, squat arches are typically Romanesque, and demonstrate the Western influence of the Middle Ages.

A memorial to the Armenians massacred during World War I.

Armenian artists engraved this ivory plaque with the various stages of Mary's journey to Smyrna.

A stylized Latin cross engraved on ivory.

Parthian temple in the ancient region of Hyrcania.

A basilica in the form of a Greek cross with several apses, topped by a stone cupola above stone tympanums.

The land of the Medes, the ancestors of today's Iranians, spread far over the Russian border, and encompassed most of Azerbaijan. In the sixth century BC, these people adopted Zoroastrianism, the religion of Zarathustra, but were then converted to Islam in the eighth century, when the Azeri cities, and especially the capital, Baku, "city of the wind," were enriched with magnificent palaces and mosques, and with fortresses that enabled the inhabitants to offer fierce resistance to the armies of Tamerlaine. Baku lies at the southernmost point of the Apsheron Peninsula; its refineries process all the oil extracted south of the Volga.

Facing page: Baku fortress.

Ancient temple of fire-worshippers.

Baku: the khan's palace.

Buffalo taking a break on the road to Kubachi.

Village in the Balkar region.

Balkar: a local potter.

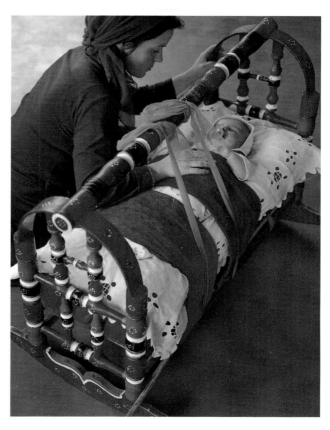

Over forty ethnic groups live in Dagestan, situated on the edge of the Caucasus. Most of them are Muslims, and they have all largely retained their traditional way of life. Dagestan's communities are isolated from each other by deep valleys filled with the oil wells that cover the region and surround the capital, Makhachkala.

A traditional cradle.

The Khoresma district. Remains of an ancient mosque.

Uzbek was a fourteenth-century chieftain of the Golden Horde – as the Mongolian horsemen were called. Uzbekistan is a vast region of mountains and deserts, stretching from the Aral Sea to the foothills of the Pamirs and running beside the Amu Darya for about 600 miles. For centuries, the caravans which wound along the Silk Road bringing cloth, tea, and spices from northern China stopped over in the cities of Bukhara and Samarkand.

Buying fruit and vegetables from a busy local market.

The cities of Bukhara and Samarkand have retained imposing mosques from their sumptuous past, though the sands of the desert are gradually encroaching on them. The origins of the capital, Tashkent, are more obscure; today it has the somewhat dreary look of an industrial suburb, most of the city having been destroyed in an earthquake in 1966.

Firing ceramics.

Ninth/tenth-century Samani mausoleum, flooded with shafts of sunlight.

Far right: preparing pilaf rice, and (right) decorating ceramic tiles.

Tadzhikistan extends along the Afghan and Chinese frontiers over the western half of the Pamirs, some of whose peaks attain an altitude of 21,000 feet. The Tadzhik highlanders, who have to endure extremes of temperature, ranging from 110°F in the valleys in summer to -20°F in deepest winter, mostly earn their living cultivating geraniums. The capital, Dushanbe, is a major center of the flower fragrance industry.

Preparing a carcass.

Cooking in the open air.

The rustic simplicity of a Tadzhik interior.

A Tadzhik child goes down to draw water from the river for his family's tea.

The land of the yak.

Probably because of the great riches lying beneath Kazakhstan's soil, there are more Russian colonists living here than there are native Kazakhs. Beneath the flat and arid steppes lie huge reserves of natural gas, oil, coal, and a wide variety of minerals – copper, zinc, and nickel – as well as rare and precious metals. The Kazakhs themselves avoid the industrial centers, preferring to raise karakul sheep and trade in astrakhan skins. They are magnificent horsemen, and still cultivate the ancient art of training eagles to hunt, sending them after wolves, desert foxes, and wild geese.

The foothills of Khan-Tengri Peak. The ancient forests, destroyed by intensive exploitation, have been replaced by a rocky wilderness.

Top: hunting with an eagle.

Karakul sheep grazing.

Preparing the meal for the fiftieth anniversary of a village elder: the goat's head is a special delicacy.

The inhabitants of Isseria love to celebrate. They are also nostalgic for their warlike past, and the men have retained the need to compare and display their skills at horsemanship, and hunting. The fiftieth anniversary of a village elder is an occasion for feasting, competitions, and traditional horse trials. Saiz is a game of skill in which the horsemen vie with each other to catch a goat, the "Saiz." The winner is honored, while the head of the animal is reserved for the most important guests.

Ceremonial slaughter of goats.

The Saiz: a ceremonial contest to win a goat, fought between Kazakh horsemen from neighboring villages.

In the second century BC, Mithradates took advantange of the disintegration of Alexander the Great's empire to found the kingdom of Pontus. His daughter, Rodoguna, fell in love with Demetrius, king of Syria, who was then a prisoner of the Parthians. Demetrius's wife, Cleopatra, was furious and had him killed. The sad story of Princess Rodoguna was immortalized in a play by the great French playwright, Pierre Corneille, while the museum of Ancient Nissa in Turkmenistan still contains reminders of the tragedy.

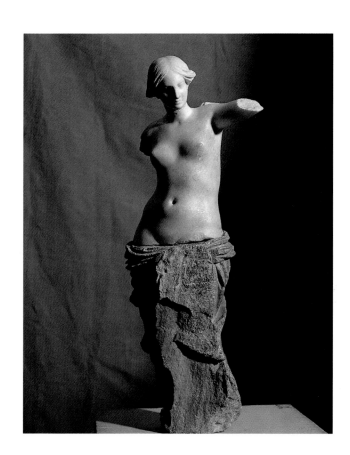

Right: ancient Nissa: marble statue of Rodoguna, and (below) stone funerary slab, both second century BC.

Kunya-Urgench: twelfth-century mausoleum of the Sufi dynasty. The minaret of the early-fourteenth-century Timura mosque is in the background.

Kunya-Urgench: the twelfth-century mausoleum of Fakhredina-Razi.

Merv: the great sixth/eighth-century fortress of Kiiz-Kala.

GLASNOST

The Khrushchev era: Yuri Gagarin, the first man in space.

In Russian, glasnost means "having one's turn to speak."
In Red Square the message is "Down with Leninism!"

The space center at Baykonyr.

Two generations separate the orbital space flight of the dog, Layka, and the latest space shuttle trials. In the U.S.S.R. the conquest of space was made at the expense of modernizing the country's industrial infrastructure. The considerable cost of the Russian space program has put the country at a disadvantage in terms of international economics. Nevertheless, Russian citizens are proud of their cosmonauts.

Facing page bottom left: Valentina Tereshkova, the first woman in space, 1970. Facing page bottom right: experiments in weightlessness.

Top and above: the return to earth.

Right: a space shuttle on its launch pad.

Modern Russia is very backward as regards agriculture, sociology, economics and psychoanalysis ... all things that the ruling powers hoped to be able to control using maxims extracted from the body of Marxist thought. However, the inquiring spirit that made Imperial Russia a nursery for mathematicians and physicists was not totally crushed by the pressures of bureaucracy, and the Academy of Science is today one of the world's most prolific state organisms.

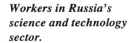

Workers in Russia's science and technology sector.

Above: an observatory.

Far right: a spacecraft and satellites in Moscow's Exhibition of Economic Achievements.

Right: a group of research workers.

The spacecraft Cosmos.

Factory workers in Moscow.

A motor truck assembly line.

A research worker and his assistant.

*Illegal garage
accommodation.*

In the Tyumen region of central Siberia, oil gushes from the earth, without necessarily bringing its exploiters the freedom from worry and trappings of luxury enjoyed in soap operas about the industry. Workers are housed in insalubrious camps, often ill-suited to the climate. Exploitation of the "black gold" has also caused irreversible damage to the forests of Siberia.

Tyumen's oil fields.

An oil technician with samples.

Under Russia's surface lies an immense wealth of minerals and precious metals: gold, platinum, silver, rhodium, etc. There are also precious and semi-precious stones, including emeralds, and topazes. In the past, in northern Siberia, it is political prisoners who have usually been forced to exploit these incredible riches, despite the appalling climatic conditions.

A shaft in a Ural emerald mine.

A stack of gold ingots.

A vast expanse of gold fields.

The Kremlin's military orchestra in the foyer of the Museum of the Red Army.

After the fall of Nikita Khrushchev in 1964, an era of lethargy, sadness, and forced-labor camps was ushered in, lasting for twenty-seven years. Writers, scientists and refuseniks protested, proving that Russia's heart was still beating, and foreshadowing the coming of Gorbachev and perestroika.

Nikita Khrushchev.
Behind him stand Souslov
and Brezhnev.

Today Mikhail Gorbachev is a lonely figure, and even his supporters are unsure of his chances of success. The Soviet Union is rising up to put right decades of wrongs, leaving an isolated Gorbachev teetering on the brink of disaster. The Union is apparently crumbling in the face of democracy and independence.

The grave in Moscow of Vissotsky, husband of Marina Vlady, and a poet and singer for freedom.

Above: a demonstrator talks to troops in Dushanbe, Tadzhikistan, 1990.

Far left: demonstrations in Lithuania during 1989 caused Gorbachev many anxious moments. Left: the military are still being called in to deal with insurrections.

Moscow's Red Square on May 9: the military march past to celebrate the anniversary of the victory over the armies of National Socialism.

Religious dignitaries lead the crowds that assembled when the Cathedral of St. Basil the Blessed was reopened for worship.

PHOTOGRAPHIC CREDITS